My Miracle in Medjugorje

A true story of one man's healing

GW00712303

John O'Connell

Oak Grove Books

About the author:
John O'Connell is a Christian mystic and the author of nine books (including this one): *My Name is John...* (1999), *Love is the Answer* (2002), *The Calling of Sinead* (2003), *The Hunger File* (2004), *Heavenly Bliss!* (2005), *The Bride of Christ* (2005), *My Life in the Eden Zone* (2006), and *Let the prisoners go free!!!* (2007). Details of these books can be found on his website at www.johnoconnell.org. He is a former student of St Columb's College, Derry, and University College Galway. He trained in Belfast as an accountant and worked in Derry, Omagh, and Strabane before a stress illness interrupted his career. He resides in Derry city.

First published in 2008 by Oak Grove Books, 7 Maybrook Park, Derry, N. Ireland, BT48 7TP or info@johnoconnell.org

232.9 /7

ISBN 978-0-9537137-8-3

DCPL0700000206

Cover Photograph: Our Lady and Jesus with their sacred hearts (Courtesy of the Cenacolo Community, Campo della Vita, Medjugorje).

Printed and bound by CPI Antony Rowe, Eastbourne

For the visionaries of Medjugorje:
Vicka, Marija, Ivan, Ivanka, Mirjana,
and Jakov

My Miracle in Medjugorje

A true story of one man's healing

INDEX

Foreword

I was not thinking of miracles when I decided to go to Medjugorje, a village in Bosnia and Herzegovina across the Adriatic Sea from northern Italy in the former Yugoslavia.

For several weeks, in fact, I had been thinking of going to Fatima just to see what it was like. I had always been attracted by Fatima because of its great secrets. But it was just that little bit expensive and so I held off from contacting the telephone number in my parish bulletin.

When the trip to Medjugorje was advertised, I was much more interested because it was that little bit cheaper and more in tune with the needs of my pocket. It was still expensive for me and it was no light decision that I made when I decided to telephone the contact number.

Nonetheless, I had become determined at that stage that I would go on a trip. So something had got to me and I was feeling "the call" that people talk about when experiencing the desire to go to a Marian shrine.

It was no mean feat for me to go on a trip in the first instance. I was a reluctant traveller in the sense that I hadn't travelled on an aircraft for over a decade, and I hadn't been away from my family for the same period. I would also be travelling on my own.

Yet I wanted to go. I wasn't looking for anything because, for reasons I'll explain later, I had my own experiences with God and I thought that any healing would come at home. I had my manic depression under control except for a very serious anxiety feeling at the top of my head that would drive me crazy at times.

It was a terrible feeling. For example, I would be speaking and suddenly the anxiety sensation pulsing at the crown of my head would interrupt my thoughts mid-sentence and I would lose my concentration and forget what I was about to say. My life was plagued by the feeling.

I could have done with a cure but I had lived with the feeling for so long that I did not think that it was ever going to go away. Yet "the call" was echoing in my mind and I felt I had to answer it.

John O'Connell

Autumn 2007

Chapter One

Miraculous healing

On Monday 28th August 2006, the midpoint of my weeklong stay in Medjugorje, something unusual happened to me. A feeling of profound irritation and anxiety, which badly affected my concentration, at the top of my head left me in what seemed to be a miraculous cure.

The feeling had been there for over six years and had been extremely bothersome to the extent that I was at pains to restrain myself from responding to its unrelenting requests to be angry and aggressive in dealing with those around me. I had become exceedingly disciplined as a consequence.

I had gone to Medjugorje with Belfast man Reggie Donnelly's group out of Belfast International Airport after answering an advert in the local parish bulletin which led me to Adele McCauley, Reggie's informal agent in Derry.

I had thought that Medjugorje was just another Lourdes or Fatima, even though I had read a fair bit about it in the past. It was strange that when I sat reading the magazine about Medjugorje in an accountancy office in Strabane, county Tyrone, where I worked as a part-qualified accountant, my eyes kept becoming fuzzy so that I couldn't actually read properly. That was in or around 1996. I actually assumed that there was something wrong in Medjugorje as if there was a demon at the heart of all the fuss about the visions and the spirituality that went along with the Marian devotion.

When I got there eventually in August 2006, I was amazed by what I found. It was far from demonic and my eyes, which had been fuzzy when thinking of the village, could now see very clearly. These visions had begun in the 1980's, which meant that they were linked to many of the things that I was going through, which also began in the 1980's and, like the visions in Medjugorje, are ongoing as I write.

I couldn't believe the state of *Apparition Hill*, where the first vision took place in 1981, when I climbed it. It was treacherous, and *Cross Mountain*, where other visions had taken place, and which was regularly climbed by the pilgrims, was supposed to be even more treacherous.

Only God could have selected this rugged, rocky little valley, I said to myself. No-one, only God, would have seen the infinite beauty of this little place, and the beauty and innocence of the local children he selected for the visions. This was a Christian paradise because of the natural beauty that would only have attracted the most Christian of families, families that knew all about poverty and need. These were not resort people who had gone to the resorts to make big money. These were simple people, who had the love of God in their hearts and the ability to live on little.

God was rewarding them as he had done the people of Lourdes, Fatima and Knock where visions of Our Lady had been seen and where miracles had been claimed.

Yet Medjugorje was set apart because the visions were still happening, and the now not-so-youthful visionaries were still getting their messages. The visionaries were mostly in their late thirties and early forties, like me, and they were so beautiful to listen to.

As I sat listening to Marija, one of the most eloquent visionaries just back from Italy where she had gone to live with her Italian husband, I was amazed at the commitment she had. She had a simple message concerning prayer, confession and not becoming attached to worldly things, and she was a beacon of light, as she spoke Italian, which was not her native tongue, and as I listened to the remarkably fluent translation of one of the guides.

I was totally overawed by the experience, and I think that it wasn't long after listening to Marija in the great yellow parish hall in the village that I had my own interaction with the forces of good that dominated the choice of the village and the happenings there.

I was sitting outside my digs just off the main street in Medjugorje, complimenting God on his choice of village and valley and rocky hills to other people I had got to know there, when I heard the distinct sound of a trumpet in the distance.

I had no reason to assume that it was the trumpet of the angels, so hailed in the Book of Revelation. In fact, it just seemed like a sound some musician was making in the village further up the street and nearer to St James' chapel. Though it also seemed as if it was just in my head. But it caught my attention immediately.

Then, almost instantly after the trumpet had sounded, a long finger from God knows where was pushed into the top of my head. It was like something that was being gently but firmly pushed into my head so that it penetrated my skull and went directly into my brain. It was like an angel had just penetrated my skull.

"That's that gone," I simply said straight away to myself, smiling. I was referring to the feeling in my head that had absolutely plagued me for over six years.

I had not been expecting anything. I was not sufficiently tuned into the Medjugorje experience to believe that it would result in a cure, or that I would get a cure.

I congratulated myself afterwards that I was very positive about the shrine, and that I was a bit like *Crocodile Dundee* in New York, like a fish out of water, and that I was totally in love with what I had found there. God must have sensed my love of the place and my enthusiasm, I mused, and he must have given me a cure as a consequence.

At the time I was totally distracted for some strange reason and I said nothing to anyone about my cure. What actually happened was that there was a dinner table situation just after the trumpet signal, finger pushing and healing. It was a slightly uncomfortable situation in that I was among strangers, mostly Belfast people, and I was really only getting to know them and them me. Added to that the food was always the main talking point at the dinner table because it tended to be mostly Croatian in orientation – Croatian culture dominated Medjugorje – and therefore it was hit or miss as to whether we would like it or not.

But the main reason for not bringing it up was that I think that I had simply forgotten that I had been cured by the time I got to the dinner table. That may seem implausible but I have no other explanation for me not jumping from the rooftops in glee at this miraculous event.

I know that I was fairly open about suffering from manic depression, because an old woman was shouting and roaring about suffering from the same affliction at the other end of our long table, and this openness enabled me also to be open. Also, I was so happy in Medjugorje that the thought of not sharing something as major as the fact that I suffered from a depressive illness to people who were to all intents and purposes unlikely to feature in my life again did not arise. Some of them were also suffering from various afflictions.

So it was not the case that I received the healing and then decided to say nothing to anyone because I would then have to admit that I was suffering from a major league depressive illness. I was open about the illness at that stage and would have been unlikely to care if I was revealing too much to other pilgrims in telling them that I was cured of something that had been annoying me for so long, and which would have effectively dominated my mood and sense of well-being for that time only I had managed to find ways of dealing with it and mitigating its effects. Despite my attempts to deal with it, it still had had an enormous impact on my life.

Perhaps the angels, who seemed to be suggesting by the trumpet that they were responsible for the cure, had dimmed my awareness of it after I had acknowledged its occurrence because they didn't want the other pilgrims to know. There is a ring of truth to this because some of the pilgrims could be very aggressive in their assertion that God was good to them.

These pilgrims would push their way into mass and gain the front seats, or seats of their choice, in order to assert that they were as worthy as anybody of God's love. There was a sense that certain people would have got jealous if you had said that God had favoured you more than them, and that their sore back, or sore whatever, which was still killing them with pain, was still not healed when they believed that they were just as good as you. They may have rebelled against God in that sense.

But most of the pilgrims would have been delighted for you. So I cannot rule out that the fact that I failed to roar that I had been cured was because I had simply forgotten as the angels made me do for the simple reason that that was how they operated in Medjugorje.

There are stories of simple cures coming out of all the Marian Shrines. There is anecdotal evidence that people have had improvements in their conditions that can neither be validated medically nor felt until they arrive home from the shrine. That may well be the way of God, not to want to overwhelm medical science with evidence of miracles that they cannot explain, or to give too much hope to people who are in a very bad way.

Yet, despite the rarity of medically-proven miracles at these shrines, there continues to be a constant flow of pilgrims who are often either seeking a cure or there to pray for someone they know who needs a cure.

So God is there. People sense him. Pilgrims know that their trip will be worthwhile in some way, even if it might be perceived by others as being in a small way. As with me, God often helps to make the load lighter of those who have very heavy loads to carry.

In that sense there may be much to rejoice about in getting a minor cure, or even a major cure, but that it would have to be contrasted against the much heavier burden that you were still carrying.

So our loving father in heaven doesn't want us to go about shouting and roaring when we are cured of something in the shrines because he feels that he has only lightened our load a little, and as a loving father he feels sad that he may not be able to do any more.

This may explain the fact that I was personally unable to share with the other pilgrims that I had received an improvement in my condition. God may simply have made me play it down in my mind to the extent that I no longer remembered the strange experience that resulted in my cure.

There was a further distraction, however. In the afternoon of the following day, while we were sitting out in the sunshine outside our digs, one of the Belfast pilgrims, whose name was Lilly, noticed that the sun was *spinning*. Immediately I rose from my seat and stood behind hers at the other end of the patio. I had been waiting on something like this for the entire trip. I had read about it happening and was delighted that I was now to witness it.

However, when I looked at the sun, I could see nothing. It was not spinning so far as I could see, and yet Lilly continued to suggest that it was. Others gathered too and said that they could see that it was spinning.

As I looked at the sun, I then noticed that an actual physical mass at the centre of the setting was now moving out of the sun and away from it. Immediately I recalled one of the women in our group telling a story of how she could see the Eucharist coming out of the sun and descending to the Earth.

I was now seeing the Eucharist coming out of the sun, and hover in front of it. It was totally detached from the sun and it seemed to be vibrating slightly as it blocked the sun's light from being seen. It was so beautiful.

'Does the Eucharist hover in front of the sun?' I asked Lilly excitedly.

'That's it,' Lilly answered matter-of-factly. She had been in Medjugorje many times before, and she was not very surprised by my announcement.

My excitement then subsided as I came to realise that this was all that was going to happen and that neither the sun nor the Eucharist was going to descend to the Earth.

I was screwing up my eyes during this incident as I was aware that it was painful to look at the sun and that it could result in damage to my sight. But when the Eucharist appeared I had let my guard down and virtually looked at the sun with innocent and gullible eyes.

It was at least reckless behaviour. It was not the right thing to do. I asked Lilly if she knew whether God would protect us from having eye damage and she replied, 'Oh yeah, you'll have no trouble.'

But I saw trouble with a capital "T" as soon as I stopped looking. Immediately I noticed that I could see a black dot on my retina, a blind spot where the sun had carved a niche for itself. I was alarmed.

I cursed Lily in my mind for having misled me. But she was getting up to make her way into the village and she was totally unaffected by her experience. I wore glasses, unlike Lilly, and I think that this may have been a factor. My weaker eyes simply could not put up with the stress of letting the sun burn a hole in their retina.

It was my good eye too, my weaker left eye being largely unaffected. I was annoyed that my good eye was affected in any way because it had served me well over the course of my life.

The feeling that I had damaged my eyes was on my mind all through the last couple of days in Medjugorje, but the feeling subsided after the initial panic and the sharp sunshine made it seem that it had gone away all together. It had not.

I got a real fright on the coach and aircraft on my way home. It was the first time that I actually saw people up close. What I saw both shocked and frightened me. I saw the faces of some of the people I looked at, specifically people who were about three meters away from me, blocked out.

There was a dot the size of about half a face at about three meters distance that meant that all I saw of people's faces, when I looked at them, was their hair, their eyes and their jaw line. It was horrendous and it really unnerved me.

The priest who had accompanied us on our pilgrimage had been comforting a young woman beside me because someone had suggested that there was smoke in the aircraft, and she had become alarmed and upset. When he had finished, I asked in an agitated mood if the priest knew about these things.

'It'll go away after a few days,' he said to my immediate relief. 'Please God,' he added, dimming my feeling of joy at hearing his initial words.

After dealing with the sheer exhaustion of the journey home and the week of the often limited sleep in Medjugorje, I began to weigh up my situation.

It seemed that I was being given a healing and a curse. I could now remember clearly the healing and was aware of the fact that the feeling in my head had gone away. But I dared not tell anyone as it just seemed so unfair that I had also been cursed with partial blindness in my good eye.

It seemed that God was asking me to accept damage to my sight in exchange for lifting the terrible sensation at the top of my head. I couldn't bare to explain that to anyone, and so I continued on my way in life without referring to my cure. It didn't seem like a cure in any case if I was still to be afflicted, even if it was a different affliction.

What could I tell people? 'Gee whiz! God cured the feeling in my head I told you about, but he gave me partial blindness in return!'

'Well, that can't be God!' they would say.

For days I was in a low level panic about this partial blindness. I thought that I was truly in a very tricky situation, and that it might mean that my sight, especially the sight in my good eye, was damaged for life. But I still held out the hope that the pilgrimage priest, who also had a reputation as a healing priest, would turn out to be right. In other words I still held the hope that the eye would return to full sight in due course.

I wasn't rushing either to get my optician to examine the eye as I felt so ashamed in the sense that I had broken the cardinal rule of all sensible human beings in relation to the sun, and stared at it with my naked eye for a prolonged period. When she did examine the eye the following February, my optician found no sign of a dot on my retina.

By then I was pretty sure myself that it had largely gone away. In September 2006, just after my trip, it had improved as each day passed, eventually to the extent that I began to regard my good fortune in losing the feeling in my head as good fortune of a miraculous nature. So I began to tell people about my "cure" in Medjugorje.

I told my mother first. While I explained to her, she indicated that she seemed to already know.

'Do you recall me telling you about the anxiety feeling at the top of my head?' I asked.

'It's gone now,' she smiled, as if someone had told her.

'It went in Medjugorje,' I added. She seemed to know.

I told my sister, Marie, and she didn't seem to realise the enormity of what had happened from my perspective. But she was happy for me.

I told everyone at a family breakfast in my brother Conal's home on a Sunday morning in mid-September. I said that I had been cured of an affliction that had tormented me for the course of this entire millennium.

Some there knew about the affliction because I had told them. Conal's wife, Valerie, knew because, as a social worker in the local hospital, she was quite sensible about these things. Others, like Conal, my father, and my other brothers David and Ronan, didn't really know since I had felt that they would not understand about the sensation or, in a worse case scenario, get the wrong impression and think that I should not be allowed on the streets while it affected me.

Ronan was a bit sceptical of the whole scenario but he came to realise that I was telling the truth, even if it was only as I saw it. But generally people were happy for me, even if they seemed to underestimate the problems that I had so dedicatedly, in a disciplined way, dealt with for over six years.

That went for others I told too. My community nurse, Margaret Devine, who I saw once a month to keep in touch with the Community Mental Health Team, was very understanding of my jubilation because I had kept her informed of the condition, even if I was a little coy about telling her that it might in some people's eyes have made me a danger to others.

There was no doubt about it. If the condition had have affected the average man, even the average man with manic depressive illness, it could have resulted in very dangerous and aggressive behaviour as they unleashed the anger and resentment at being afflicted in such a way. It could have resulted in criminal behaviour or, in the case of the manic depressive, behaviour that would have resulted in him being sectioned under the mental health legislation, being a danger either to himself or to others.

I never let it get me down. On first experiencing it, I repressed all anger as it arose and eventually it simply stopped arising so that I was calm and unaffected on the surface. But this took great dedication and great discipline, and probably some good fortune. My good nature was tested in every way possible.

In late September, almost a month after receiving the cure, I felt that I had to thank Our Lady in some way for her intervention, for in effect making my life bearable again. At that time, I had got into the habit of reading the weekly religious newspaper, The Irish Catholic, which I had read on and off for quite a few years, and so I decided that I would put a little advert in it, thanking Our Lady.

"Sincerest thanks to Our Lady of Medjugorje for a miraculous cure," the advert read. The advert was signed "John O'Connell, Derry City." It went in to the newspaper in late September or very early October 2006.

By that stage I was in the middle of writing a short book called, *Let the prisoners go free!!! The Case for a Christian Justice System*, which was my slightly amateur, but more perfect because of that lack of a professional tone, plea for an end to the subservience to the Old Testament in the laws of our western countries and for the implementation of Christ's teaching in those same laws.

The important thing to note about the book was that it was written with a clarity that I had not been able to achieve since I developed the devastating sensation six years before. It was, in fact, the first book that I had written without feeling the sensation since *My Name is John...*, my first book which concerned my manic depressive illness.

It was a revelation to me. My mind was so focussed, and I was able to think so clearly, that I think that the short book was the best analytical one that I have ever written. It was as if the holy spirit had invaded my mind and was guiding me to do God's work. I had always tried to do God's work when writing my books, but this one was different.

It was the first time that I had actually specifically addressed a biblical issue and therefore it was the first time that I had had to challenge the orthodoxy of the Church and give a radical interpretation of the Bible. I came to the conclusion that the Bible was the Book of Good and Evil, the evil appearing through a deviant God in the Old Testament, and the good appearing in the teachings of Jesus Christ.

Orthodoxy suggested that it was the same God in both the Old and New Testaments, the God of Israel. Yet the deviancy of the Old Testament God had to be challenged and I made that challenge in my book. My book was very logical and very well argued, but was not a learned text, and not meant to be, in the sense that I was not a Bible expert.

But as a manic depressive, I was an expert in behaviour that was not usual. I could assess someone as deviant and someone as good, even if they were supposed to be God, and I knew that I was on to something. All my thoughts of the previous lifetime fell into place due to the clarity of my thinking and the ability that I now possessed to assert my opinions.

I was a new man.

Chapter Two

My mother's influence

When I had finished my book, I was truly feeling on top of the world in comparison to how I had felt in the immediate past, and it was all to do with the healing in Medjugorje.

Yet there was another aspect to it building up as the months progressed. I was getting up earlier in the morning in order to write extra pages of my book and, when a first draft was finished, I was very keen to complete the editing work.

It was a strange way of working. Most weekdays I would do an hour from ten in the morning to eleven, working on my book. Then I would get a lift to the gym with my father, who happened to be going in the direction of the gym. I had been going there three times a week since the end of the previous June, and it gave me a feeling of health and well-being.

I would return home on the bus for lunch, and after lunch I would do another hour on the book. I would then take the bus into the city centre and make to walk home again in what had for a much longer time than the gym been my mainstay in terms of exercise. It was a forty minute walk that I usually broke in two by stopping in the local Sainsbury's supermarket café for a coffee.

When I returned home, which would have been at about four thirty, I would have completed another hour in the spare bedroom I had made my office, working on my book. After dinner I would have returned to the office for another hour's work.

Everything revolved around the book when I was working on it. I had a deadline and that was to make sure that the book was ready to go to the printers by the end of October. It was a short book and it required only basic research since I had almost everything in my head, and so it was for the most part only a matter of writing down my opinions on the subject.

So achieving the deadline was not really ever going to be a problem. Especially since I was giving it so much time and effort, making sure that I was going to be ready in time for Joe McAllister at the Guildhall Press to do his part in translating the text from *Microsoft Word* that I worked with on my personal computer at home to the *PDF* format used by the printers.

I dedicated the book to Our Lady of Medjugorje, explaining in the introduction that I would not have had the clarity of thought without her miraculous healing.

After a week or so in the Guildhall Press, Joe called me to suggest that we complete the work one afternoon and, after paying a small fee, we were on the road to the printers. I posted the disk together with a cheque to cover costs and Antony Rowe Limited in Eastbourne, England, told me over the phone that it was going to take six weeks to return the printed books to me. I was then to sit patiently for the books to arrive in early December.

The gym was boring but challenging. I arrived there in my shorts and slippers, and immediately got changed into my t-shirt. I then did twenty minutes on the exercise bicycle, twenty minutes on the walking machine, ten minutes on the rowing machine, and fifteen minutes on the exercise bicycle again in order to finish.

I was not really pushing myself too hard in terms of pace but it was a demanding routine for an excessively overweight forty-one year old man.

There were moments, however, when I got glimpses of the reality that I was probably pushing myself too hard. Thoughts would pass through my mind that I was manic depressive and excessive exercise combined with excessive mental stimulation might result in me becoming unwell again.

I had alarm calls too. A thought would pass through my mind suggesting that I ask myself where all this was going.

'What's going to stop this?' I would ask myself.

It was a serious thought to pass through my mind. I had had a good run without the usual symptoms of manic depression. The last time I had the usual symptoms of my illness was in 1997 when I had been put on a low dose of antipsychotic medication. This medicine had taken away the symptoms of mania altogether, and I was left with merely the psychological effects of having suffered seven major episodes and a few aborted episodes of mania over the course of the previous eight years.

However, I also had a depression in the second half of 2000 A.D. and that may have been seen to be part of my illness. I didn't regard it as such. I regarded as a result of an assault by my doctors, which I didn't take very well.

But all in all things had been good for as long as I cared to remember, and I was leading quite a normal life. The only major feature in my life that wasn't normal was the fact that I wasn't working in a paid job.

But the way I saw it was that I *was* working: I was doing *God's work*. Every book, and I had just finished my eighth, every article and every letter to the newspapers highlighting our cause, was *God's work* and one day I would be rewarded for that work.

It crossed my mind that perhaps the healing I was receiving from God was my reward. It was a fleeting thought, but one that warmed my heart.

'What's going to stop this [excessive activity]?' I asked myself on occasions, and I was beginning to get worried. The healing was allowing me to do too much too soon, and this was causing me concern.

The sense that I was out of control in terms of my energy levels, both physical and mental, and not getting enough sleep, or at least no where near as much sleep as I used to get, worried me. My sleep worries might have been unwarranted in the sense that my adrenaline levels were higher than normal and this was providing me with much more motivation than I was used to at that time.

Yet, as Christmas 2006, approached, I was quite concerned in a fleeting way that I was running into trouble.

From a manic depressive's perspective, trouble meant either more tablets or a stay in hospital. I wanted neither, even if the tablets were not usually too much trouble to take. But I was fed up with the mental health service, and every time it got another claw into me it sounded the death knell for my desire for a normal life.

I resented with every bone in my body the mental health service's intervention in my life. Doctors made me feel nauseous, and although I didn't hate them, I tended to think that they had no right involving themselves in people's lives.

They had a job to do, but in mental health their rights over patients were quite extensive, even absolute, in cases where patients had neither the will nor the education to object, and they used these powers on occasions.

In my own case they had regularly subjected me to sections under the mental health laws, and I found this neither amusing nor enjoyable. They had their reasons, of course. I was ill in their eyes. In my eyes, I was not always ill in these situations, and that had created tensions between me and those doctors who had had the temerity to carry out the abuse.

The doctors were not at one with me in concluding that the reason that I was in a psychiatric hospital was because God wanted it, and not because they had ordered it in sectioning me.

I had always held that view of my illness. I had always said that I was in hospital because God had made it seem that I was ill, creating the circumstances for a simulation of the symptoms of illness.

At first, doctors suspected me of being a paranoid schizophrenic because I was showing fears that the IRA was going to kill me and because I was seeing things on the television that were not rational. In my defence I had been told by a friend that the IRA were going to kill me and, as for the television, I was seeing things that were irrational to others but which seemed perfectly appropriate to me at the time.

I was seeing a lot of coincidences on the television, many of which, I felt, related to me and my life. I suspected that it was God communicating with me, but I had absolutely no way of communicating that to others, even those in my own family.

My diagnosis was eventually determined as manic depressive illness and when I heard it, after four episodes of illness, I felt that

God was actually trying to discredit the doctors who had made both of these diagnostic determinations on me.

That analysis seemed to make even more sense now that I was healed of the worst effect of my illness. It confirmed to me that God was with me right from the very moment that I had had begun to exhibit the symptoms of mental illness to those around me.

I could recall those moments in Belfast when things started to go wrong, and I knew that I was not alone.

I realised that there was something manipulating events when I began to suspect that there was a grand conspiracy against me. Even in the context of an illness, which I did not accept that I had, I knew that some force was manipulating events.

Doctors may say that that is the way that everyone feels when they're experiencing the symptoms of an illness. But I knew it was not natural.

It was too perfect for a start. At least it seemed too perfect. Nothing had been left to chance. The difference between my experience and an illness was that everything had been outside of my control, so I was not manipulating events. I couldn't explain this to the doctors.

So far as they were concerned it was the same old story of a patient who had feelings that there was a conspiracy against him when there was no conspiracy. In other words, the doctors seemed to believe that I was paranoid.

But I believed that "they" were out to get me. It wasn't only in my mind. I had strange experiences that indicated to me that I was being conspired against. It was strange but true.

My best friend told me that "they" were going to "shoot me dead" in a crowded bar that had just filled up with young, working-class, men and women, who I had never seen in this upmarket bar before. It alarmed me the next day but at the time, even though I had only drunk a single pint of beer, I was disinhibited and emotionally unmoved by the incident in any negative sense. On the contrary, I even laughed and joked about it.

Even the next day I was not fearful. I had wanted to prove that something was going on and I felt that I had got to the bottom of it when the IRA had made a threat. So I had played the incident up a bit. But my best friend denied telling me that there was a threat when he was quizzed by my father.

I suspected that he was being manipulated by the paramilitary grouping when I heard this since the IRA would never admit publicly to intending to assassinate the son of an SDLP councillor. They would certainly never admit to having botched an attempted murder and that meant that it was sensible to assume that they would never admit that they had told my best friend that they were going to kill me.

But there was more to it than that. I was having a ball of a time in our home where I was supposed to be becoming ill. Most of the time in any case I was quite happy about all the attention I was getting.

However, it was not natural. It was not a situation that anyone could accurately describe. I was separated from all the goings-on as if I was meant to know that everyone was simply doing as some force told them to do.

Everyone seemed involved from my best friend to my father and mother to my brothers and sister. Even my elderly aunt, Myra, my mother's sister, entered our living room to try to assure me that everything would be alright.

She seemed to be suggesting that I would be alright when events fully transpired and the implication seemed to be that I was in for *a joyous surprise*.

Was I now experiencing this "joyous surprise"? Was it in the experiencing of a miraculous cure that meant that I was one of the few people alive to know that there was a God? It seemed that this was a very pertinent moment in that respect.

Christmas came and I was happy that I was one of the few chosen by God to whom to reveal his existence. I had a fair idea that he was there. But it confirmed what I always thought, that I was not on my own and that God was prepared to help me in my work.

There were times when I was not fair with others around me. At least I was not fair in an objective sense to an objective observer. I would have felt that I was being quite fair but on very rare occasions I was given to lose my temper and lash my tongue out at people.

On one such occasion just after Christmas Day, I lashed my tongue out in a slightly aggressive way at my mother. It was only a minor argument, and not one that would have annoyed my mother too much. But it was something that I noted.

I was concerned that I might be losing it again in the sense that I was prepared to be unfair to my mother when the problem we were discussing wasn't her fault. Yet we had a few rows from time to time and I was only really thinking aloud when weighing up the row. But it wasn't a good thing to be unfair to my mother. She was a special person.

I had witnessed her influence when, in the midst of a manic episode, I had taken her to see the father of a man who had broken my nose in an assault. She sat silently in that meeting in his home, but she was listening to every word, mainly to ensure that I didn't become aggressive to this man.

But she had witnessed one of the tactics of this man in dealing with those who he considered not to be one of "his own". Instead of being sympathetic to my plight in developing what he knew to be a major league depressive illness after his son had assaulted me and then harassed me on several occasions over the course of a year, leading people to believe that I was a likely candidate for becoming ill, this recently-retired man instead took up the cudgels on behalf of his family member.

'You both had drink taken, hadn't you?' he pointed out in a rhetorical fashion, as if he was a judge and jury.

'No, we were just very tired,' I suggested in reply, defining the cause of the incident from my perspective. I would never have let myself become involved in such an incident but for the sense of tiredness after a long summer of professional exams and waiting for results. But his son represented a danger to others for other reasons and the drinking had merely disinhibited him, allowing him to show his aggression.

Drinking was no excuse in my mind. I was not aggressive when I took a drink. His son had assaulted a doctor's son in a local nightclub a couple of weeks before attacking me. His problem may well have been *the demon drink* in that he was going through a rough patch and he could no longer cope with his problems. In fact, his younger sister had twice made some advances on me while quite drunk and I felt that she was heading for a drink problem, if she did not already have one. Some people changed when they took a drink. These two siblings were among them.

But their father was a smug bastard. He had no hesitation in giving his son an excuse. But there was more than one person in the audience that day. He couldn't get away with it in the way that he got away with similar attitudes that he had displayed when my friend had asked him about a car crash that his son and two of my friends were involved in.

The car had been driven by his son's friend and, after his son had allegedly egged on the driver for several miles to speed up, he skidded out of control and crashed straight into a lamp post. His son couldn't say or do very much as he had helped cause the accident. But his father defended his son and the son's friend, suggesting that my friends had taken a lift in the car and were therefore morally obliged to put up with their minor injuries and the trauma. The implication was that they should be grateful for the free lift and not make any claim.

I was against them making any claim too, but for different reasons. I knew the car driver from school and he was a nice guy who had been egged on by the man who had broken my nose. But I advised my friends to be sure that they had a winning case – even though they had had quite serious minor injuries in the traumatic car crash – before they took any claim because I knew that they would never live it down if they lost. They eventually decided to make a claim, which they won, because the driver had failed to contact them after the accident and had instead travelled to Dublin, making my friends feel that he was deliberately avoiding accepting responsibility for their injuries.

Another occupant of the car, a friend of my assailant, made enquiries of me in Belfast, where I was living then, asking me if my friends were, like him, considering making a claim. He had found out that he had chipped his shoulder bone and was in pain from his injury. But he subsequently decided not to make a claim as his family was friendly with the driver's. It didn't stop him thinking about it, of course.

When my friends went to inquire as to whether the man who had subsequently assaulted me was going to claim too, his father told them that they were lucky to have got a lift that night. But any sensible human being knows that you are responsible when you are at the wheel of a car, no matter if you have charged a fare or not. You cannot endanger people's lives through reckless driving, and then rely on the fact that you had been kind to them in offering them a lift. That type of kindness can cost lives.

It was the same strategy again for the father. Always stand up for your own, even when they are in the wrong. He was a deeply perverted and flawed man, who had in my mind brought up a deeply perverted and flawed son who also tended to stand up for wrong even when it was perfectly clear that it was wrong. Always defend the fort, son, I hear a *Davy Crockett* figure say.

My mother would have been disgusted with him. She would have known that he was deeply prejudiced man, a man who defended those who were "in the club", the family club, even when they were in the wrong.

My mother had brought us up, and my father held the same views, with the attitude that we own up to being wrong when we were wrong. My mother would often have erred on the side of accepting that we were wrong even when we weren't, just to show neighbours that she held respect for them and to send out the signal that no nonsense would be tolerated.

But she was a kind and good mother during our childhood. In our early adulthood we would not have given her any reason for criticising us or, more pertinently, for being ashamed of us. We were never responsible for assaulting anybody else, and would therefore never have been in the situation that that vulgar man was in.

When we left him at the house that day he looked healthy and focussed. The next I heard of him was about eight months later when they were burying him. He had died from cancer on Christmas Eve.

I sensed that my mother had some part to play in that. Her presence had been important when I flagged up the old bigot for bringing up such a deviant son. At the time, as soon as he gave his justification for the assault, fearful that I would get angry and lose control in my manic state, I just told him that his family where a credit to the community and to him. Most of them were. His "black sheep" son was a liability, but that went unsaid. He knew what I meant.

But it was a tragic death for his family. He had just retired from his job and was set to enjoy a long retirement when my mother and I had visited. However, I knew what we had brought during our visit. I had been frantically praying with my mother in the Nazareth House chapel just before we arrived. So we had brought God to him, and it was judgment time.

I could just imagine him at the time of his death insisting to God that he and all his family and all his friends should get into heaven because they were all upstanding members of the community. When God questioned this, he would naturally ask the question, "Have you been drinking?" Well, they say it's hot down there.

My mother's presence was symbolic and not a derivative of witchcraft. She hadn't cast a spell on the errant man. She had simply mortified him into embarrassment. I believe there are triggers in the human psyche that recognise when you have been beaten. He was a beaten man that day we visited, and he became vulnerable to an attack from cancers as a consequence. His bigotry had been laid bare and the will to live had left him in an unconscious sense.

My mother got the justice that every mother who has been affected by acts of physical violence on her flesh and blood wants for herself and her child. She witnessed her son's assailant's father attempt to justify an incident that had begun a series of incidents that may have led to the ill-health of her son and the destruction of her child's life.

She had had to help to pick up the pieces of her child's broken life and she was entitled to be less than sympathetic to the denial and the attempt to blame her son for the actions of *his* son.

In the final analysis, God had taken the old man on Christmas Eve, denying him the privilege of seeing the day of his son Jesus' birth, and slighting him in the process.

My mother was entitled to suspect that it was a judgment and, if she was the kind of person who thinks these things, she might even have believed that she played a role in delivering what was *poetic justice*.

It was justice in another sense too. My assailant's mother was now left without a partner in her old age and perhaps this was the greatest insult of all. God was leaving her on her own, and so he may well have been saying that she was the person who was most to blame for her son's delinquency, and not her bigoted husband.

I realised in a conscious sense that the death had God's calling card written all over it, and I knew then that my mother was cherished by God. She was cherished because she was a good person. There was nothing more to it than that. But she had "sent" a man to his death because he was not good in her presence and had indeed demonstrated a dishonesty that would have turned her stomach.

So I was even more careful with my mother after that. God was watching over her and protecting her interests. He was at least protecting her family and ensuring that any slight against her or them was responded to in kind.

On 28th December 2006, I found out that God was listening to me as I argued with my mother. Well, with the benefit of hindsight, I realised that he was listening to me. That day the anxiety feeling at the top of my head returned.

I was shocked, but not annoyed. I realised that there was more than a hint of truth to the fact that it related to my mother and the argument between us. However, it was also exactly four months after I had had the cure in Medjugorje, which was on 28th August, and I realised that there was another message coming from its return.

'I'm being called back to Medjugorje,' I told my mother, not wanting to let her feel that she could get one up on me through God's intervention.

'Well, you'll just have to go,' she said lovingly. My mother knew that I had another mother in my life. She had interceded to give me the cure and I was going to find out if she would intervene again. But the next trip would not be until the summer.

Chapter Three

A healing lost

During those initial few minutes after the healing had been taken away from me, I was devastated that God could be so cruel. Nevertheless, I felt a special bond with him and I knew that he would not leave me to suffer the burden on my own. He would help, as he had always helped.

However, the sensation of anxiety and the pulsing pressure on my head felt worse now that it had come back. Perhaps that was because I was genuinely more anxious. But it was working away on the top of my head as if it had never gone away and I sensed that I was in for a hard time before any further healing, if there was to be further healing.

That was the question. Was there going to be any further healing? Was God, in his infinite wisdom, going to bring me back to my former self, before I had had the affliction in the year 2000 A.D.?

Or was he really angry at me for having the row with my mother? This may have indicated to him that I had not changed and was therefore unworthy of the cure that he had provided. There was a ring of truth to that assertion. I *was* unworthy, even if I tried my best most of the time to be a good person.

There had to be a certain degree of anger at the heart of God in order for him to take away a cure.

Yet in my heart of hearts I knew that God was God and he knew what type of person I was when he granted the cure in Medjugorje. He knew that I was flawed like every other person on the planet and he knew that I was the kind of person who would sin from time to time.

Therefore it seemed that the taking away of my cure was part of his plan for me, and furthermore he knew that by taking away the cure at that very moment when I was arguing with my mother it would signal to me that it was because I was sinning when I shouldn't. His withdrawal of the healing was meant to have maximum impact in that sense.

Yet all of these thoughts seemed to indicate that this was the plan that God had set out for me and that it *had to, just had to*, involve further healing when I returned to Medjugorje.

The fact that the withdrawal had taken place exactly four months after the healing assured me that Our Lady was central to my experiences and I trusted in her.

I prayed, and still do, every day to Our Lady of Medjugorje using the prayers that she had indicated in her messages to the six visionaries. I pray seven Our Fathers, seven Hail Mary's, and seven Glory Be's each day as she requested.

I would go, and have been going ever since I decided to go to Medjugorje in June 2006 before my August trip, to the area dedicated to Our Lady in our chapel and say the "triple seven" prayers that I had found out about on an Internet site.

So I realised that Our Blessed Lady would not let me down. I knew in the way that someone who had had God in his life all his life would know that this was not going to be the last of it. It would have been some kind of big joke to heal someone and then take away that healing when they had finished with him; and so I was aware that it was not the case that God had given me the clarity to write a book, a book that he wanted, and then decided to dump me. That was not the way of God.

Nevertheless, I am but mortal, and I was pretty annoyed at times when I thought of the effort I had had to put into that book, and how it seemed that it had stressed me to the extent that it might have led to a recurrence of my illness. I was pretty pissed off at God in those moments and I would have used his name in vain in my head for having put me through that ordeal.

Yet it was more than that. It seemed as if God had been using me to write the book, a book that would have consequences for the whole of humanity, and then discarding me as if I was a piece of dirt.

However, my understanding of God was that he was not like that and so I held fire in badmouthing him. In fact I told very few people about the loss of my cure.

Obviously it was bad for me to have to admit that my cure had been withdrawn. It was embarrassing even if most of the people I told about the cure would probably think that it was all in my mind in the first place.

It was a difficult part of the body to need to have cured. There was no doctor's opinion on the affliction in any real sense, except to suggest that it was some kind of "hallucination", an opinion which didn't tie in with my sensations of pulsing and waves, which were physical, on my head.

My doctors had been coy about the sensation, not really ever expressing a forthright opinion. Yet my consultant psychiatrist had ordered a brain scan on an MRI machine when I asked for one because I felt that it may be as a result of an injury to my head. I was also concerned that it may have been the result of the effects of a brain tumour.

I felt initially that the sensation was caused by a bang to my head in hospital where I had collided harshly with a shelf above my seat. The sensation had started not long after that and I was concerned that I had done some damage. But I was clutching at straws at that stage and the sensation was all the time raging away without hindrance from my medication or from any medical intervention.

The sensation was, as a consequence, very real to me. It was extremely irritating and extremely substantial. It seemed to know exactly how I would be annoyed most and went ahead and did it.

Nevertheless, when the sensation returned I never once doubted that I had been given a miraculous cure by divine sources. After all, it had happened in Medjugorje, a Marian shrine famed for its peace, inspirational atmosphere and the occasional miraculous healing.

But I had also got the memory of a trumpet call and a long finger pushing down into my brain just before the healing and so I was sure that there had been a miracle. I didn't doubt that just because the miracle had been withdrawn.

They say that God moves in mysterious ways, and I felt that I knew exactly what was meant by that at those lonely moments during the early days of the return of my anxiety sensation.

I felt some relief, too, when the feeling returned. I was relieved that my episodes of manic depressive illness, with the corresponding hospitalisations, were not going to return. I had feared that this would be the case if I continued on with the excessive energy and the mental sharpness that the healing of the sensation had allowed.

So I was not completely unhappy that the sensation had come back.

The strange thing about the anxiety sensation and its relationship with my illness was that it was as if having the former formed a barrier against having the latter. In other words, the feeling in my head seemed to act as some kind of controlling agent in keeping my illness at bay.

This meant that I was not troubled in the six years or more of having the sensation with any kind of symptoms of mania, whether it was excessive physical activity or excessive mental energy.

In the early days I had suffered from the symptoms of depression, but it was a reactive depression in my opinion relating to abuse that I had suffered at the hands of the hospital system and my former consultant psychiatrist.

But my general feeling about the anxiety sensation was that it was a way of preventing any other symptoms arising. It did this by keeping my mind permanently focussed on the symptoms of the manic depressive illness, such that I never forgot that I had the illness and thus was not tempted to risk doing anything that would change my stable mood.

Many people who suffer from repeated episodes of mania will, like me, have had the problem accentuated through forgetfulness. In other words, they will fail to remember the symptoms of elation or mania as they arise again and again and the symptoms will progressively worsen each time they recur until the sufferer arrives at the stage where they are no longer able to control themselves and they will inevitably end up in hospital.

Having a sensation at the top of your head constantly reminds you that you have an illness and that you cannot afford to drop your guard. I would even go as far as to suggest that it prevents you from dropping your guard in the first place so that you live with a low level of tension all the time.

Nonetheless, the anxiety sensation was just that. It was anxiety to me, even if I never really knew why I was supposed to be anxious. It was deeply unpleasant, even profoundly disturbing. It had been so since it first occurred and, for the most part, I bitterly resented its return.

As I say, the hardest part for me to accept was that it may have been necessary for it to return because I was struggling to maintain my mood.

The good and caring God who brought me the cure was undoubtedly aware that it was not the right time for me to be healed. He was, I hoped, going to bring me further healing the next time I went back to Medjugorje.

Next time I was going to ensure that I didn't take any risks with my health after I received the healing. There would be no high pressure books written by me next time.

Ultimately I knew that God was with me on my journey through life and ultimately I knew that he wasn't punishing me for the row with my mother or any other of my many sins by withdrawing the healing.

He was doing what a loving father would do when he saw his child struggling for his sanity because he was beginning to become ill with a condition that was easily more serious than the anxiety feeling on his head that he had in the final analysis actually coped well with over the course of the previous six or more years.

So, yet again, I felt the protective hand of God in my life, even if the consequences of the sweeping stroke of that hand were difficult to accept. But I had always had that kind of relationship with God. It had never been an easy relationship and it always challenged me to the utmost.

Yet his love and protection had always been there.

Chapter Four

A child's God

There was a certain similarity between Jesus and me in our relationships with God. He had had such a beautiful time in his life healing the sick and teaching large numbers of people before God had effectively "kicked him in the teeth" by insisting that he had to be crucified.

Jesus' story was beautiful too. Too beautiful. He also had to be brought down to earth with a tremendous thump that had resulted in his death. The bubble had to burst. There was never anything simple with this God.

I was pretty sure in that sense that it was the same God who asked so much of Jesus who was now asking me to accept that he was taking away my cure. He had asked so much of his son by guiding him to his Cross.

Yet there was always the resurrection. So I was not completely overwhelmed by my predicament. I was sure that there was a way out, a way to find the ultimate peace with myself and the world.

One of my first memories as a child was of my father, my older brother and me strolling on a march and of me telling my father that I had to go to the toilet. He took me to my granny's nearby. It was that God again.

The march we were strolling on was the famous 5th October 1968 civil rights march on Duke Street, which every Derry man, and some from further afield, seems to have been on, despite the fact that there were only a few thousand people there that day. It was nonetheless a prestigious march, more so for the fact that the RUC had waded into the crowds and effectively announced to the whole world, in front of television cameras, that the Troubles had begun in earnest.

And I had to go to my bloody granny's for a wee! It was typical of the God who gives and then takes away that I had to go for a leak when all the action was taking place and policemen were battering the crowds with truncheons.

Yet again, of course, God would claim with a certain level of unquestionable truth that we were safer as young children, and my father would be safer too, if we got offside before the brutality began.

It might have changed my entire life if God had allowed me to see that brutality. It might have made me violent, or even timid, and yet as it turned out I was one of the few people there who was unaffected by the events of that momentous day.

So God had been right yet again. But the protective hand of God was hard to take at times and this was one of those times.

There was also another parallel to this march when, on 30th January 1972, the day Derry's *Bloody Sunday* took place when British paratroopers had opened fire on an anti-internment rally organised again by the civil rights people, killing thirteen mainly young men, with one man dying later.

It was again a large part of the modern history of Derry, and I had missed out on attending the march because my mother felt that it was too dangerous. My father was on the march, but he wouldn't take me on it because of my mother.

In any case I was just six years old and marches were by then boring, so I wasn't looking to get taken to the march that day. There were in fact very few children there for a combination of these reasons. But no—one could have foreseen the devastating and brutal violence of the British soldiers, or the significance of that cold, damp winter's day, before it happened. Afterwards "everyone" seemed to have seen it coming.

But the protective hand of God was on my shoulder, ensuring that I wasn't put at risk. Nevertheless, I would like to have been there when my people were being attacked and brutalised by an alien army. But God in a sense sheltered me from seeing at first hand the evil actions of the British army.

A few weeks later, in mid-Spring when the weather was better, I might have been tempted to go along with my father just for the *craic* and I might have potentially witnessed my father being shot dead. It would have transformed my life and made it nearly impossible for me to have stayed out of the IRA ranks, which had swelled as a consequence of that profoundly wicked day.

It was never easy to accept the verdict of God's protective hand, but it was understandable in the context of my young life which evolved into supporting the non-violent politics of the Social Democratic and Labour Party (SDLP) through the influence of my father. For me our politics have their origins in Jesus Christ's teaching, so the thought that God was in our lives was quite natural.

We grew up in a young boy's paradise with a primary school behind our park and a recreation area surrounded by trees in front of our homes. The recreation area consisted of two grass football pitches and an improvised all-weather pitch for when the grass pitches were unplayable. Surrounding the recreation area were further special schools for special needs children, a nursery school and even a Mormon Church, which brought God to the district, even if no-one I knew attended the ceremonies there.

The changing facilities in the recreation area happened to be burned down during the early days of the Troubles in an effort to bankrupt the British government, demonstrating that evil men were conspiring to destroy our little paradise.

God's protective hand hadn't extended to preserving the changing facilities, and we were quite annoyed at the republican vandalism at that time.

Yet I can see now that what actually happened afterwards was that fewer and fewer outsiders came to use the facility because the changing rooms had been destroyed. Fewer outsiders meant that there were more opportunities for the children of the area to play on the grass pitches.

So sometimes good could come out of a dramatic situation, and the evil that men do can inadvertently be for a reason, the reason being to make things better for others.

Therefore God's protective hand was often there in my life without me knowing it.

In reality, I was not the sort of person to assume that God was responsible for this and that in my life. The assumption that God is always there is a totally self-absorbed way to go about your life, however much people believe it. Nonetheless, I don't know anyone who totally believes that every aspect of their life was guided by God. It may well have been the case that their life *was* guided, and I believe that all our lives are influenced greatly by God, but not every burp and fart.

Our parents were the real heroes of our childhood for having chosen to live in our park. My mother always says that she needed to have a "green area" in front of her home and so it was decided that they choose this particular park. She had grown up opposite her local church and so she may have valued the green area in a sacred way in her mind, giving it the status of hallowed ground.

That hallowed ground was dishonoured one day by me, but only in our back garden. At the age of seven, I set a hedge on fire in our garden which raged in a small way for several minutes and got me into some trouble. I didn't like the type of hedge and so I decided to burn it a little. The fire spread out of control and, despite my best efforts, I ended up having to enlist the help of my father to put the stubborn blaze out.

So God was with us in our choice of area, but he was not always extending his protective hand to keep us out of trouble. He let us get on with what we wanted to do, however perilous. Yet there was always a sense that we would never have been allowed to do anything that would have endangered our lives.

In any case, in the era of Martin Luther King and President John F. Kennedy, our parents had chosen to live in an area which allowed *their* idealism to shine through. They were a new generation of wise and idealistic parents who wanted things to be better for their children than it was for them.

I sense the protective, and the loving, hand of God in the choice of my parents of our park. They moved there in 1964, several years before the outbreak of the Troubles, and it was a place on the outskirts of the city that turned out to be quite "protected" from the worst effects of those troubles.

We were some distance away from the nearest centres of commerce and the local bank, which attracted regular trouble, and so we were not confronted in any real sense with the very worst incidents of the conflict.

Nevertheless, we had our moments.

There was a shooting in our park during an election day in the early 1970's. An IRA man shot blind through a high garden hedge and riddled the school assembly hall exterior with bullets. The school had been serving as a polling station.

The shooter had advised the older boys to lead us away from him and to get out of the way themselves. Then there was a crackle of gunfire for a few minutes as we lay on the grass at the other end of the park.

No one was killed, so we weren't really too worried by the experience. On the contrary, it was extremely exciting for us to witness real gunfire.

Then there was a bomb at the corner of the front row of our park, six doors away from us. It shattered our windows and almost killed a neighbour. The target was an RUC man out on foot patrol and he was seriously injured, though he didn't die.

We were watching a television programme when the car bomb exploded and were just about to open the window blinds when it went off. So we could have been badly injured, even scarred for life by the attack. Pieces of car were strewn all over the place, from front gardens to rooftops.

So we knew that God would allow us to experience all of the world, the good and the bad. He would not intervene to prevent us from seeing the gorier aspects of his planet just because they were gorier. His guiding hand would allow us to see *the real world*.

There was always the sense in my mind that there was a God and so I was not all that concerned that I would be allowed to go to pieces.

But it was certainly not the situation as in Jim Carrey's film *The Truman Show* where his character was totally in a false man-made

43

situation in which everyone observed him on a television show. We simply had a sense that there was a God but that bad things still happened to good people.

There was at the heart of our identities a sense that we were good children and that God was real to us in the sense that he was helping us to lead happy lives.

My happy life at school was disrupted within a few weeks of it beginning when I got a homework for the first time. I told my mother that we weren't getting any homework because we were so good in class, and then we got one. I was mortified. I had set myself up for a fall and all I could think of was doing the homework in our bathroom so that my mother wouldn't see me.

But my teacher noticed, mainly because I had used an old purple crayon to complete the homework, and she enquired with my mother about getting a pencil. I was mortified again.

So God didn't prevent me from being mortified. He didn't help me to save face when I made mistakes. He, like the loving God that he is, allowed me to make my mistakes so that I would learn from them.

The pattern emerging is of the hand of God guiding my life to happiness, but when I had achieved it he let me make mistakes and experience even the most dangerous of situations so that I would know that my life was natural and normal and not contrived. And there was exactly nothing contrived in our lives. It was all real.

There was a *real* tag fight one day in the park with the "rough" boys at the back of the park being set against our gang. I had to rough another boy up in order to gain my colours. God didn't stop that even though it was not a Christian thing to do.

So God was in our lives and it was a strange relationship. He gave us on the one hand a really beautiful upbringing and on the other hand he allowed things to happen that contradicted the view that we were Christian people.

However, that was his way.

It was the way that it had always been. God allowed us in effect to believe that there was no God by allowing us to make mistakes. Some of those mistakes had resulted in boys dying in their childhood because they fell from trees or got knocked down by cars. Yet God didn't prevent us from climbing trees or crossing the road.

The only way that God could ethically, and I believe he works by ethics, prevent us from taking risks was by ensuring that our parents instilled in us a cautious attitude when it came to taking risks.

I was always cautious about taking risks. From the first time my mother showed me how to cross the road, I would never allow myself to be rushed or jump recklessly in front of a car.

Fortunately for me, I knew the power of the car. One day I had jumped from an embankment at the side of the road and landed awkwardly, striding involuntarily onto the road. A car coming from behind me had screeched to a halt in an instant, but it managed to bump me in the backside. It was sore but my pride was hurt even more. I walked away, red-faced with embarrassment.

These narrow-miss experiences would have accentuated in me, if any accentuation was needed, that the God that I believed in would not be there for me every moment of the day. I'm sure it was the same for everybody else. This created a tension in our lives and it was consequently difficult to argue with those who suggested that there was no God.

If there was a God, how could he allow so-and-so to fall from the tree up in Steelstown, or wherever, to his death.

'We're on our own,' some boys would suggest.

Strangely it wasn't very often that they would suggest it. We were quite happy in our lives, living beside a prime amenity among decent people, who had little in the way of pretensions about themselves.

The police were rarely in the area, never mind there to deal with crime. The only major incident that got me into trouble with the police occurred on the other side of the border and was when my friends and I had gone to Burnfoot, seven miles from Derry, to do some fishing.

On the return journey, which we had arranged to do on foot, having been given a lift down by our parents, we noticed some tin cans on the side of the road. We decided to do our bit for the environment and throw them back onto the road, whence they came.

A passing motorist alerted the Gardai, who had a station nearby, and the oldest boy was made to go back and lift the cans off the road. It was amusing but it was also symptomatic of a happy, crafty childhood that I suggested that no-one give their true name when the Guards asked. All the boys then made up these fantastic names that the big policeman would never be able to check before we got back over the border. In any case, we hadn't been breaking the law, only keeping the environment clean.

Yet I was a sinner. I sinned against my mother and father by stealing sweets, and then money, when I was a young boy.

I began innocently enough by stealing chocolate and other sweets. But it graduated into stealing money, and I was very furtive and crafty at doing it. It became bothersome after a while and I really was glad that it ended when it did, around about the age of eleven and before I went to the prestigious Catholic grammar school, St Columb's College.

God was the only one I would tell about the stealing, because I presumed he already knew. Yet it was symptomatic of a God who was allowing me to learn from my experiences that I was actually allowed in the first place to sin against my hard-working parents. He didn't regard me as a bad person, just someone who had gone off the tracks and who he was confident would return to those tracks some time soon.

God set out deliberately to convince us that he wasn't there by letting us experience life threatening situations and near-misses. But in the sense of sinning against God, he always allowed us to return to him eventually. We are all mortal. We can all sin. But God is there to allow us to be ourselves when the time is right.

I felt the protective hand of God in my life when I gave up the stealing, even if, yet again, the consequences of the sweeping stroke of that hand were difficult to accept in the sense that he allowed me to sin in the first place. Yet, as I have suggested, I always had that kind of relationship with God. It has never been easy but it has always been challenging.

Yet his love and protection has always been there. The most loving way to protect someone was to allow them to make their mistakes when it didn't matter so much, so that they wouldn't make them when it did matter.

God was allowing us to test the limits of good behaviour and even exceed them just for that reason. We were truly the children of God.

Chapter Five

A youth's God

There were times when I thought that the protective hand of God was nowhere to be seen such as on the occasion when I had almost been blinded in one eye by a "spear" thrown by one of our next door neighbours' sons. We had been throwing makeshift spears at each other over the dividing hedge as part of a game and I had simply decided to look to see if one was coming.

It was one of those situations which had the effect of making us believe that there was no God in the world and that we had to be absolutely careful to ensure that we took control of our own lives.

Yet, because it was so precise an injury that did only a little damage, it had an interesting feel to it. If the wound had have been millimetres lower it would have resulted in me losing my eye and then belief in a just God might have been difficult. Nonetheless, it had the feel about it that God was there, even at that very precise moment, and in the context of that very dangerous location for an injury.

In other words, there was a sense that the fact that it was as near a miss as possible may have signalled that the hand of God was at play. This would not have been the case if the spear had landed on my toe and bounced off my shoes.

So there was a sense that God was at the edges of life, guarding the perimeters and both helping us to survive tricky moments and creating a plausible deniability to questions of his own existence.

That became a theme of my life after my early childhood.

My father became a councillor on Derry City Council in May 1977. He was elected as an SDLP candidate on the seventh count and went on to serve his constituents for twenty-eight years up until May 2005.

He was mayor of the city in 1982 to 1983, and something happened in the run-up to his election that should have served to heighten our feelings about God.

The protocol at that time was for mayors to serve as deputy-mayors first, and this meant that my father should have served his year as deputy before becoming mayor. But the DUP deputy-mayor, or the mayor in waiting, was making strong soundings that were disagreeable, even offensive, to the Nationalist community. So the SDLP decided to drop her as mayor and elect my father instead.

There was going to be some hullabaloo when she found out that she was being dropped, and the unionist community were probably going to withdraw from the council for a time in protest. My father would then have become a hate figure to some unionists, and to the odd crazed Nationalist who wanted to make his party out to be hypocritical for not sharing power, and he would not have enjoyed that. We were bracing ourselves for trouble.

Then the strangest thing happened. The deputy mayor died suddenly just days before the election for mayor and the SDLP, as the largest party, decided to stick with their plan without telling the unionists, who never suspected a thing. My father had avoided being a hate figure and what would have been a troubled mayoralty turned out to be fairly uncontroversial.

It seems such a blasé intervention by God in the life of our family. It was so large and so monumental we were bound to think that it wasn't an intervention at all. God would "never" choose one side over another. He would "always" remain neutral and faithful to the gospel of the equality of all human beings. He would "never" do something so large that would affect one family over another. Nothing would convince us that there was anything more to the death than coincidence.

Yet something was to happen just before that time which set my mind thinking that something had to be guiding my life. I was to suffer a bout of chicken pox that resulted in me missing the term exams that were used by the school authorities to stream pupils into better classes.

The only exam I did was Religious Education and it was another giant coincidence that this intervention in my life resulted in me honouring the only subject that really mattered later in my life when all was said and done.

It also resulted in me being left behind in classes which had their fair share of underachieving boys and so it would seem to have been another intervention on that level. God was telling me not to desert my own people, not to consider myself as a part of the elite, and I never really forgot these urgings of God, despite what others might say, in the years to follow.

So there was a sense that I was receiving messages, albeit in a subconscious manner, during the course of my life.

I received another very clear message that even I sensed at the time was divinely influenced when I took up boxing at the age of fifteen. I was slightly uncomfortable with the whole scenario, which I had only involved myself in reluctantly because a friend had asked me. So I was looking for a way out towards the end of the season.

The way out came in a mysterious way through an illness I received on the day I was to fight in the Ulster Championship final. I was struck down with a virus, but felt that I had to fight that day. I lost and that was my short career in boxing effectively over. Had I been well, I feel that I would have won comfortably and then the pressure would have been on me to come back to the club for training the following season.

I somehow sensed that it was a sign urging me to give up the boxing. In any case it effectively broke the back of my boxing efforts and made the process of withdrawal from the club much easier.

Nevertheless, God was working in mysterious ways, and I was quite alert to the possibility that I had got a sign that in fact contained the message: give up the boxing.

In retrospect now, I can see the gentle guiding hand of God nurturing me in the direction that he wanted for me. So why did he allow me to box at all?

It was strange that the first boxer I ever fought was a Jew and I knocked him down three times. There is something to that which was beyond me at the time, but which later becomes clearly a message that there was something Biblical about my life and its direction.

I was to receive another more substantial Biblical message in the ensuing period that gave us a momentary sensation that God was with us in a big way. Again it involved politics, the sense that not all individuals were equal in the eyes of God, and the sense that God was choosing one group of individuals over another.

About the time I was boxing in 1980 to 1981, I was told by a friend at St Columb's that the letters of the name Ian Paisley, leader of the DUP and now the First Minister of Northern Ireland, came out at 666 on a certain numeric alphabet.

There was something very mysterious about the way I was told which was as if I was being let into a great secret that no-one else knew about.

'If it was anybody, it would be him,' I told my friend, implying that if anyone was to be the Antichrist then it would be Ian Paisley.

I told another friend about the discovery and his reaction was exactly the same as mine. He told a priest in the school, telling him that it was my discovery, much to my annoyance, and that was the experience over for me.

Of course, I did a little research at home and was very interested for a relatively short while in the matter. I calculated a few other names, including my own, and I read the passages in the Book of Revelation but was not sure what they told me. I was content to let the matter rest there.

But God was not content to do that. The matter was raised again in my second year at university in Galway.

Politics was a major part of my life in those days, and still is to some degree. I was always discussing political matters with my friends and these matters mostly related to the violence that was tearing apart the North of Ireland. It was a conflict that, like all violent conflicts, had turned people away from politics and was attracting an element of hardliners who relished the prospect of using violence on others to get their way. In the Catholic community they were represented by Sinn Fein, led by Gerry Adams.

It was "personal" between the leaders of Sinn Fein and me. I had almost been killed at the top of a ladder putting up SDLP posters in the Bogside, again God failing to intervene to make it seem that he really wasn't there. However, he was there alright or I would most definitely not have survived. It was that harrowing.

Pieces of furniture, including parts of a cooker, were thrown from the high flats above me as I stood at the top of the ladder trying to secure a poster to a lamppost. I was shocked.

Then the cowardly young men who threw the implements at me appeared at the door of the flats and, as a bit of bravado, I bid them to come over to us a hundred metres away. I didn't know what kind of animals I was dealing with. These were the henchmen of Martin McGuinness, Sinn Fein vice-president and now Deputy First Minister, who were guarding a giant Sinn Fein poster hanging on the side of the flats, and they didn't like my actions one little bit.

They couldn't get me because I lived at the other side of the city, so they got a fellow SDLP poster team member who was known to them and who was there when I had made hand signals at them. They broke his arms and legs in what was a well-publicised assault on an SDLP election worker. But it was one of the many brutal attacks that these animals were responsible for during the course of elections and at other times, both as members of Sinn Fein and as members of the IRA.

So I was developing a personal animosity to Sinn Fein that depended wholly on my belief in God and his values. I knew that Sinn Fein were not Christian.

Moreover, I knew that the SDLP were the party of Christianity in our conflict zone with its social democratic ethos and its emphasis on social justice. Our party was the party of non-violence, virtually the only major party that took that line, and that was very much the reason why I, and many people, had come to serve it.

There was something going on in my mind when I went to Galway. There was an experience in the first few days that set my mind thinking of the justification for being there. A bird fouled on me. This was not an ordinary bird. This was *a dazzling white seagull* that seemed to glide down from the clear blue sky, where it was the only bird present, and let go of its load just above me. It then flew back up into the sky.

'And it didn't even say, "This is my Son, the beloved, in whom I am well pleased,"' I said immediately, with just a moment's reflection, sensing the Biblical importance of the incident and the parallel with Jesus. It was as if I was being initiated into some kind of God's squad.

Nonetheless, I had been joking in saying what I said to my friends. Yet there was a secret me, and that that secret me was one hundred per cent certain at that moment that I was the second coming of Christ. But I stress the words "at that moment" because afterwards, as normal life took its course, the certainty disappeared and I would not have consciously associated myself with that line of thinking at all.

However, one particularly beautiful spring day in late February of my second year, the mid-point of my course in 1986, I had the most earth-shatteringly exciting experience that anyone could imagine.

I found that Gerry Adams' name came out at 666, just like Ian Paisley's, on the same numeric alphabet. I was dumbfounded. I was on my own in the little flat inside a local family's home I shared with Cormac, also a Derry student, when I found out about the Sinn Fein leader's name. I tried other names again but without a match.

This was a major coincidence. It was not only a coincidence in the sense that the name worked out at 666 but also in the sense that it equalled Ian Paisley's name on the same numeric alphabet. Two names together spelled out trouble for the North and I was fearful that something major was going down.

Statistical probability, a subject that I had just scored 95-100% in my term exams, indicated that this was so unlikely as to be impossible in the case of the leaders of two of only four main political parties in the North. God was being blasé again. He was demonstrating a barefaced ability to tell us something that seemed so obvious that it was true and yet also so patently "obvious" that it could not be so easy to work out.

Yet anyone who knows the ways of God – particularly around Marian shrines – knows that the truth is often given into the hands of the meek or the uneducated or the poor before it gets as far as the rest of the population. It is certainly never put into the hands of the rich or the powerful or the Biblical scholars. It may eventually find its way into the hands of these people, but not before the poor have been allowed to filter out anything that *their* God would not have been the source of.

So it was perhaps a case of the poor being allowed to filter out anything that would not be pure or innocent or without the scent of money and material things in passing on any message that they received from God.

So why didn't I simply pass on this message to the elite? I did in a sense. I told Mark Durkan, now leader of the SDLP and MP for Foyle who was then SDLP leader John Hume's assistant, and I also told some Sinn Fein members in Galway, who I didn't regard as among the animals that were part of their party up North.

Why didn't I tell a priest? I had no doubts for a few days, and to a less pointed extent for a few months, that I had come across something that was going to change the world. But even with that certainty I had other problems. My flatmate was having some kind of breakdown and he went missing in the middle of my term exams. So it turned out not to be the wholly beautiful life experience that I had hoped for when I went to live in the flat.

It wasn't simply that God again, giving with one hand and taking away with the other. This was more a matter of handling me, of giving me the strongest sensation possible that I had come across a Biblical revelation, and then creating a diversion so that my mind somehow dismissed the importance of my experience and especially any personal relevance it held for me.

So at the time I had the experience of working out the number of Gerry Adams' name, I was suffused with feelings of personal significance that depended heavily on the absolutely beautiful experiences I had had in Galway to that date that made me feel part of that world and – this is crucial – part of God's plan. I was having that kind of experience when I worked out the numbers and this had its zenith in the previous few weeks when I had worked for my flatmate, Cormac, as his campaign manager in attempting to get him elected as the student vice-president. It was absolutely wonderful and I loved the experience.

Yet all that changed and the sense that my life in Galway and to that date was beautiful in any way changed with it. "All changed, changed utterly, a terrible beauty was born," to quote W.B. Yeats, and this dark and hurtful beauty changed my life at that time. It also distracted me from my experience and made it seem that the likelihood that God had given me some vital, strategic Biblical information was remote.

It was undoubtedly God's way of handling me because he had plans for me; I was to find this out soon enough when I made my way to work in Belfast.

Other things happened too that meant that I was not feeling the protective hand of God on my shoulder. During the summer after my experience in Galway our house was attacked by republicans intent on warning us not to do anything with the coincidence of their leader's name coming out at 666. Windows were smashed at the front of the house and the assailants ran off, never revealing the reason they thought they were doing it.

At the time, we thought it was to do with my father being a councillor, but later I was to attribute it to my discovery in Galway that I had told very interested Sinn Fein student members about. Yet it was another reason for me losing the sense that God was in my life and that only good things happened to me, a feeling that would have led me to conclude at times that the experience in Galway was from a God who was giving me the most marvellous of times.

As an aside to this story I have to reveal that there was an interesting revelation when the picture of the attack appeared in a local newspaper. If you turned the photograph upside down, a reader rang in to say, you could see the face of the now Saint Padre Pio.

Nonetheless, this experience and the illness of Cormac were preparing me for a life that was going to be difficult at times in the years ahead. It was not going to always be idyllic.

So I never ended up going to a priest.

I wish I could say now that I was wrong to have assumed that something major was going down because of my experience in Galway, but there are things that still must happen which mean that Gerry Adams and Ian Paisley, now the two most prominent players in the politics of Northern Ireland, will be generally regarded as the two beasts of the Book of Revelation.

At the time I was only aware in a vague way about the fact that there were *two* beasts, and not *one*, in the Book of Revelation. But I was to become increasingly aware that such a situation existed as my life progressed from my innocent student days at Galway to my more earnest days in Belfast.

Nevertheless, those were beautiful days when God seemed tangible at fleeting moments and when the effects of these fleeting moments were to warm my heart for days and months after.

God was in my life now, and he was gently introducing himself like someone you meet at a wedding, whom you meet afterwards by chance and somehow manage to get very close to. My God was protective and caring, and absolutely beautiful. But he was also difficult to deal with.

In Galway we were at the beautiful stage in my divine experiences and in the general experiences I had there from when we went on holiday to the capital of Connaught as children, to the camping holidays as teenagers, to then as a student, where the protective hand of God was on my shoulder. But the other side of the covenant I had with God was to come. It was to prove equally earth-shattering but much more long-lasting in its effects.

My parish bulletin of 12th August 2007 suggests that God is as complex as I am suggesting: "The disciple advancing in faith has to learn that God is in the dark experiences of life as well as when all is bright and cheerful. In the night-time of faith it can often be difficult to pray or be hopeful. Yet God is in the night of faith as in its daylight, when everything seems to be going well."

It is food for thought and the fact that the parish published it just as I was writing the first draft of this chapter of this short book means that it is a terrific coincidence.

God is mysterious. He wants to show us his love but doesn't want us to wallow in that love for long. He sends along terrible trials just to show us that he doesn't want us to depend on him for anything other than the most pure level of true love that we human beings can achieve. He doesn't want to demoralise us. He wants us to learn to survive, it seems at times, without him.

He certainly doesn't want us to come to believe that he exists with the kind of unrealistic certainty that some religious people profess to have.

We cannot always be certain that God is there. We can, if we're really insightful, often be certain that something is there and that it is capable of influencing our lives in every way possible, both good and bad, and that it is acting in a very profound way.

If God reveals himself to us, we can be certain that he is utterly good. When God has revealed himself to us, and we're beginning to wallow in the experience, then God will bring other more negative experiences to bear on our lives, so that we forget the reason why God was making it seem that he had revealed himself to us.

It's called "life" to other people, as they struggle through the ups and downs of their existence. But insightful people know that God is there causing the downs as well as the ups in order to ensure that people don't get the wrong idea about him. The reason is clear.

He wants people to know that they're not obeying the will of God, as given in the teachings of Jesus, when he sends us the plagues. When we're ready, he'll reveal himself to everyone. But that depends on everyone taking seriously the rules of his son that are in everybody's interests.

It might just be the case that God is ashamed to admit that he created this human race and the reason he won't give the religious the right to beat the arguments of the scientists is because no-one, especially some of the religious, are taking Jesus Christ seriously enough.

So *God plays God* in the lives of his children, making them happy and sad, and may do so until we take Jesus seriously in our actions as well as in our words.

Nonetheless, I was to find with a great deal of certainty while I was working in Belfast that there are exceptions to the rule that God doesn't reveal himself totally to human beings. I was also to discover the extent of his seriousness in wanting us to change. The change as it related to me, I was to find, had begun in earnest in Galway with my discovery of the fact that Gerry Adams' name came out at 666. I was to come to realise that I was an important part of God's plan.

I had the wisdom as the Book of Revelation suggested: "This calls for wisdom. If anyone has insight, let him calculate the number of the beast, for it is man's number. His number is 666." (Rev 13:18)

Chapter Six

God of the Catholic Church

A fierce struggle was going on in Belfast for the hearts and minds of the Catholic population when I arrived there in 1987. The Bishop of Down and Connor, Dr Cathal Daly, was leading this campaign against IRA violence and Sinn Fein complicity in that violence.

The SDLP, after years of harassment and intimidation from republicans, had a very weak presence on the ground in West Belfast, and the Catholic Church was feeling threatened by the strong growth in support for Sinn Fein.

Led by Bishop Daly, the Catholic Church there took a very hard-line stance against republican violence. This led to walk-outs at mass and other protests. These protests were a means used by republicans to intimidate the priests of the diocese, who were simply following the teachings of Jesus Christ on non-violence when they spoke out against the IRA and their supporters in Sinn Fein.

I freely admit not to have considered while I was living in Belfast whether Bishop Cathal Daly had been acting on my "numbers" discovery in Galway a couple of years previously. But considering it now, Bishop Daly did seem to take enormous risks in attacking Sinn Fein. Rather than being patient with his flock, he risked at the very least alienating a large section of the Catholic population and turning them permanently against the Church.

Yet Dr Daly was a highly intellectual man and he would have realised that the reality was that these "alienated" people were in any case part of a rebellion against Christ and his Church. So Dr Daly would have opposed them anyway, regardless of my discovery, and that meant that the news that something big was going down, involving the Book of Revelation, had probably not reached the Catholic hierarchy.

Yet there was something unusual about Bishop Daly's appointment as Archbishop of Armagh and leader of Ireland's Catholics when it happened in 1991. It seemed to indicate that the whole Church hierarchy was supporting his campaign to topple Sinn Fein. It also seemed to have worked.

In 1992, Gerry Adams was to lose his seat as MP for West Belfast to the SDLP's Joe Hendron. Some would say that a tried and tested path had been tread by the Catholic Church. There had at least been a parallel when in appointing Pope John Paul II from his Polish base the Church had effectively bolstered the cause of the opposition there and ensured that the entire edifice of Communist rule in Poland came to an end. This had in turn led to the collapse of communism in the Eastern Bloc, with one country collapsing after another in a *domino effect* until they were all gone.

So it could be argued that the Catholic Church leadership, after a long and arduous battle with Sinn Fein in West Belfast, had done what the Catholic Cardinals had done after Pope John Paul's struggle with Polish communism in appointing him to Rome. They had created popular support for the cause of peace and justice and against violence and Marxism by appointing Dr Daly to Armagh. This would have influenced voters in West Belfast to at least momentarily abandon their rebellion against Christ and the Church because it demonstrated that there was support for their Bishop's stance, and it had helped to topple Gerry Adams, the leader of the rebellion, from his position as MP. Within months of his defeat Gerry Adams was talking of an end to the IRA's campaign, a "complete cessation of military operations", and so Pope John Paul's desire to elevate Dr Daly may be seen as having proven fruitful.

Some say that "what goes around, comes around" in a karmic sense. This seems true as the Pope who was elevated by the profoundly wise tactic of hitting the enemy at their weakest point seems to have used the same tactic himself in appointing Dr Daly as Archbishop, helping to end the campaign of violence that had confronted the entire people of the North of Ireland for a quarter of a century.

There is an uncanny parallel in any case and I was very taken by Dr Cathal Daly's promotion to Armagh.

The reality, of course, is that if you asked a member of the Catholic Church hierarchy about Cathal Daly's elevation, and you attempted to imply that they knew that it would lead to the ending of the IRA campaign, you would get a blank look.

You would probably also get a blank look if you had asked any of the Cardinals involved in elevating Pope John Paul II about their decision and you put it to them that they were really intent on ending communism.

It may seem that that is how the Church operates with all those wise and scholarly men at the helm. But someone like me, who has seen God in action, and who knows that big things are happening at the moment in the world, knows that the hand of God was at play both in the case of the elevation of Pope John Paul II, who turned out to be the most popular Pope in the history of the world, and in the elevation of Archbishop, later Cardinal, Daly.

Both these measures were necessary, firstly in creating the circumstances for the defeat of the *beast* internationally, or Godless communism and, secondly, in the context of the North of Ireland where the *beast* was advocating violence generated by the support of that same Godless Marxism and a challenge to Christ and the Church.

So when the Church says that it is fighting evil, sometimes it is more accurate to suggest that it is providing a vehicle for God and his angels to fight that same evil.

I couldn't help but note that the same God who was helping – then obstructing – me in my life was present at the very head of the Holy Roman Catholic and Apostolic Church, to give it its proper title, and had in fact given us the most extraordinary man as Pope for two decades, only to challenge our assertions that God was with us by then giving that same great man symptoms of what was probably Parkinson's disease. It was not supposed to happen to the man who was infallible in matters of faith and morals.

But it was typical of my God, the God who had given Jesus the most remarkably beautiful ministry only to have him struck down by the crucifixion. It was the God who gave and then took away, and I was desperately hoping as the summer of 2007 approached that he would be in a giving mood.

In 1988, back in Belfast, I was involved in an incident that would in the end signal a monumental change in the course of my life. I don't think that it in its own right caused my life to change dramatically, but I think that most other people around me were to come to believe that the incident had changed my life irretrievably.

In late summer 1988 there was a fracas outside an upmarket local bar and I was head-butted sustaining a broken nose.

It was an unfortunate turn of events that led to the head-butt. I had been out with a couple of friends for a meal and a few drinks and by the end of the night was quite well on in drink. I was not the sort of person to get aggressive when I went out and had a few drinks.

In normal circumstances, I would just have gone home after the long evening, or we would have gone looking for women for a bit of *craic*. But this night we happened to run into my assailant, who was himself by his own admission quite drunk. The difference, of course, between him and me was that he was aggressive that night, and had been aggressive on at least one occasion in the previous few weeks when he had also broken the nose of a doctor's son over what seems to me to have been a relatively trivial matter.

He was also aggressive in discussions with me over political matters on several occasions and I seemed to be a magnet for him because he disagreed with my politics. He was a supporter of the old Nationalist Party, then called the Irish Independence Party (IIP), a rump suspected of tacitly supporting IRA violence that had been obliterated by Sinn Fein when they entered politics in the 1980's.

He didn't like my assertion that night, when we had got talking, that the reason Sinn Fein had wiped out the IIP was because they were perceived to have stood for the same values in relation to their policies.

Nevertheless, my assailant had "sensed" what I was really saying and he "knew" that I was saying that the reason the IIP failed was because they had been perceived to have supported the IRA, and the electorate were now getting Sinn Fein men who were in fact the real IRA. The electorate had quickly disposed of the phoney IIP and replaced them with the real thing, Sinn Fein, a party that openly supported the IRA and never had any qualms about it. The IIP had facilitated their demise by ploughing the same republican furrow of the IRA and Sinn Fein, in defiance of the SDLP, for a number of years.

So my assailant was in effect humbled by our discussion and he left me at the bar, after several long and bothersome minutes where he was clearly at least affected by alcohol.

So shouldn't I have been wary of him?

I would be failing in my duty to any young person who has an interest in politics, particularly non-violent politics, if I were not to advise them of the pitfalls of even engaging casually in political banter with someone like my assailant.

I would advise them to be wary of anyone who has assaulted anyone else either wrongfully or when they perceive themselves to be in the right. My assailant felt that he was right to intervene in a relatively minor dispute between his friend and the doctor's son and head-butt him.

Nevertheless, the fact that someone deals with a dispute in such a way is not to be lauded, especially when that same person is mouthing on about politics and has shown a very great interest in those matters.

My assailant was someone who had lost the ambition to go into politics that his great interest in such matters implied. Such men are dangerous, and they are at their most dangerous in the aftermath of having made the decision that political life was not for them. Here was someone verbally abusing a politician's son about politics in a bar a matter of weeks after head-butting the son of a local GP. His career in politics had just ended and he no longer mattered. I was foolish to speak to him.

I *was* wary of him, but because I was a little   disinhibited due to drink, I let my guard down to an extent. I was a big man, with almost exactly the same build as my assailant, and so I was not afraid of him.

Outside, after the bar had closed, his friend referred insultingly to my father and to the incident when I had been at the top of a ladder, putting up an SDLP poster, and almost killed. I was about to respond to him, but only verbally, when my assailant began a rant.

'You're Sinn Fein,' I roared, harking back to the basis of our argument inside the bar. The night air had just hit me and I was feeling the drink for the first time in a long time.

Feeling the blunt reminder of the argument he lost inside the bar, my assailant marched fifteen yards forward and stood in front of me, threatening me. He wanted me to say it again. But the march forward was legally the assault, and he added to it by causing actual bodily harm as we struggled and I took my gaze off his face for just an instant.

He had lost the run of himself. This was a dangerous man who had now no interest in political life even though he prided himself in browbeating all the other potential political candidates off the field. This was a bully, who had no chance of a political career, and he was totally out of order.

My assailant was now fully supportive of the Old Testament value that it was "an eye for an eye". From previous arguments I knew that one of the reasons he despised the SDLP was its non-violence that came from its forward thinking views on forgiveness. But his values were ego driven. He felt that he had the right to respond violently to me even after his provocation to me, which involved him harassing me that night and on previous encounters. In truth he has exposed for me the sickly truth about the Old Testament law of "an eye for an eye". It is really about provoking your enemy into reacting and when he reacts you then feel *aggrieved* so that you feel justified in "retaliating". His *grievance* means that it is all about his ego that ignores his own bad behaviour and concentrates on the behaviour of the enemy. That is why there can be no basis for "an eye for an eye" in Christ's teaching or in any Christian law.

He would have remained a potentially very dangerous bully were it not for the fact that I took it upon myself to challenge him in the ensuing weeks and months about his actions.

I made him confront himself and realise that his actions left him open to be destroyed, not just in the sense of a political career which was over for him in any case after both assaults, but also in the sense of his legal career which he was about to embark upon in the days after the assault. In short, he had left himself open to be blackmailed.

More importantly, of course, I had to ensure that he realised that people were hurt by his actions, and lives potentially destroyed, because he could not handle a problem that his friend told me he had, which seemed to be quite serious. So it was not appropriate that he took out his anger and tension on other people.

Potentially, of course, I had the ability to end his career as a solicitor, and it may seem remiss of me not to have simply gone to my own solicitor friends and began legal action. I could have got significant damages for an injury to my face. A solicitor friend, who was there on the night in question, told me that he could get me £18,000. But I baulked at this.

The money would have come in handy as I struggled on a trainee accountant's salary. But I was careful that I didn't create a lot of enemies by making my assailant out to be the victim by ending his career in law. That might not have gone down well in certain quarters. He was also a lawyer and lawyers are notoriously hard to get a conviction against in courts in any jurisdiction, but particularly in the crony-world and the objectively-corrupt world of the Northern Ireland court system.

In any case I was having a ball, taking on my assailant. I kept in touch with him over weeks of negotiations, negotiations that proved fruitful for me in the sense that I humbled him again and again. The truth was that I didn't need to do anything in order to humble him: he was totally feckless and kept making mistakes.

In the end, however, when I could no longer contain myself because, by almost threatening to assault me again, he had effectively given me the opportunity to end an agreement we had reached the day after the assault, I reintroduced charges with the police.

I left it at that. This was a more bothersome time as I wondered whether he would lose his career in law and whether his friends would blame me. So I didn't appoint a solicitor and I didn't make a second statement to the police. They never asked for one, so I can guess that they were never very serious about embarrassing the legal profession in the city.

I got a telephone call six months after introducing charges to tell me that the DPP had dropped all charges against my assailant. I was happy at that.

My assailant had stopped trying to intimidate me at that stage, and so far as I was aware he hadn't assaulted anyone else. So it was a minor achievement in the sense that he had assaulted two people in the space of two weeks and then stopped totally for a year. I had done my job in the eyes of God, I found out later.

Nonetheless, there was the moment to come when he was going to try to re-assert himself in a masculine way. Over a year after the assault, he approached me in a bar. I was ready for him, having watched him the whole night keeping his eyes on me. He asserted himself; I responded as a mature person who still had a future in both politics and accountancy, and he was dragged away by his friends.

Three months later, we shook hands twice at the urgings of a mutual friend. The first time he withdrew from the handshake midway through it. He was suspicious of my motives and it seemed that he actually believed that *he* was the victim at this stage, so hard a time had I given him.

The second time we shook hands he had raced minutes after the first aborted handshake from the other end of the bar, as I say he was a somewhat feckless human being, in order to shake hands with me. I don't know what changed his mind, but this guy was something to behold.

A friend of his lived in the same house as me in Belfast and asked me after all this whether I had done one of those SDLP training courses in America. The implication was that I had totally outsmarted my assailant, using tactics that I had learned in America's hot political cauldron.

Nonetheless, my friends knew the truth. I had been stressed by the events surrounding the assault which happened in the midst of professional examinations and my friends knew that it had taken a fair amount out of me. My assailant had in many senses threatened my dreams of a political career and, even though he acted predictably and stupidly, he had used up precious energy when I was studying for my exams.

In the context of God, I had been given the most wonderful experiences in Belfast. There were dark moments too, but apart from the assault, I had come out of it quite well.

For example, I was having one of the most interesting and professionally enlightening times that any trainee accountant could have. I had learned quickly about spreadsheets and I had been able to get involved in the preparation of business plans and financial modelling. We had prepared business plans for various businesses including a glass manufacturer, who had received millions in grants from the government, hotel entrepreneurs, nursing homes, manufacturing firms and even a condom supplier. These plans were then taken to the banks and the government where they received hundreds of thousands of pounds of funding.

It was extremely interesting and very few trainee accountants could claim honestly that they had been given first class work during their training period.

Of course then the assault happened and it was a case of *the Lord giveth and the Lord taketh away.* It was my God again, the God of Jesus and of Pope John Paul II and of the Catholic Church.

The Lord was just playing with me to that date, I was to find out. Soon he was to get really serious.

Chapter Seven

God of the ill

I had had quite a beautiful time both in Belfast and especially in Galway. Even before that in Derry I had had a good life. I wanted for nothing and I had been able to repay my parents with good results in my secondary school exams and in my university exams. My parents never really had any worries about me, they were to say later.

I was the strong type who never bended or broke. I was resilient. Even in my wars with my assailant I had stood firm and allowed him to make mistakes rather than being too adventurous. It was my strength and my weakness.

It was my strength in many ways because it meant that as long as I worked hard and kept doing the things that I had learned to do, I was on the right road. No-one could ever knock me off that road. I was supreme. That's why my assailant played into my hands by perpetually trying to outsmart me. No-one could outsmart me, of that I am sure.

He was trying to outsmart someone who was simply waiting on him each time and who was too sure of himself ever to be worried by threats and intimidation. I was a working class boy, brought up with some middleclass attributes, but I was also extremely solid. I was not fragile in the way that my assailant was. I would not bend with the wind and concede to him just because he was trying to intimidate me in front of my friends or trying to bully me into seeing things his way.

I was my own man. I did things my way. I was happiest doing my own thing, using whatever charms I had to coax a woman into my life, or studying for my term exams or my professional exams. When I set out to do something, I usually did it. I always did my best, but rigidly so, such that I maximised the effort put in.

Therein lay my weakness. I was rigid in the sense that it is sometimes better to bend with the wind a little so that when it does blow harshly, you do not break completely. So I could have been a little more rubbery and a little less brittle when it came to dealing with stressful situations.

I could have bended a little with my assailant and accepted that he had simply made a big mistake on the night in question. I could have dropped the charges with the police and let him have his fun at my expense. But others would undoubtedly have been assaulted.

However, one of the things that motivated me, and contributed greatly to the rigidity, was the fact that I wanted to follow my father into politics, or at least I wanted the option to remain open. That meant that I had a permanent focus and that that focus was in a forward direction, and that incidents like the one with my assailant simply held me back from achieving my *raison d'être*.

I was not ambitious in the sense that I would have gone out of my way to make an enemy. I was not going to be a career politician or a snotty-nosed businessman. I was not like my assailant in the sense that he would have made it his business to try to humiliate people he regarded as not as good as him. He had what I would call a deviant, but massive, ego that drove him to insult his way through life. Even though his ego was massive, it was also probably the product of self-loathing; some kind of inversion of his true self had taken place to achieve this perverse situation.

I had slightly lower self-esteem than might have been warranted by my achievements in life to that date. So the contrast between my gentle diplomacy, born of lower than normal self-esteem, and his ruthless thuggery, born of a giant ego caused by inverted low self-esteem, could not have been greater.

The fact was that most people would have had lots of minor problems throughout the course of their lives whereas I was going to have either very few problems or I was going to snap and break completely. That was due to my rigidity in no small measure.

And I did snap not long after my moral victory in the dispute with my assailant.

This is where God really entered my life. It didn't seem like it at first. It just seemed as if there was this unduly large conspiracy and I was at a loss as to what it was about.

It began at a wedding where the parish priest indicated that he "knew" me. He could have been saying this because he wanted to make us believe that he knew everybody, or just a local councillor's son; but he unnerved me because he was the brother of my parish priest. My parish priest was also my assailant's parish priest, and my assailant was close to the Catholic Church through his father.

I wrote a letter to my parish priest, admitting that I had felt "shame and embarrassment" at the dispute and waited for his reply. This was the beginning point of the "breakage" of the brittle material I was made of.

There was a coincidence at mass on Easter Sunday, less than two weeks after my letter. The priest mentioned "shame" and "embarrassment" in his sermon. There were other curious moments involving people present at the mass and I was quite concerned that the Church had taken sides in the dispute with my assailant.

I went to Belfast to get away from the possibility of having the confidentiality of my letter abused. As the train pulled into Botanic station an elderly couple looked anxiously at me as if they were there to keep an eye on me and to ensure that I had not gone to Belfast to harm myself. It was yet another coincidental communication of a couple who were clearly concerned about something.

On Easter Monday I tried to telephone the Bishop of Derry, Edward Daly, but he wasn't available. Later, a woman followed me in Ormeau Park, where I had gone to get relief from the mild feeling of stress that was building up over the sense that there was something going on.

At lunch on Tuesday, my friend Peter smoked profusely and seemed quite agitated. His uncle was a Jesuit priest and I assumed that he might have heard something of a dispute between me and the Church, particularly the priests in Derry, from him.

One of my housemates thought that I was becoming "paranoid" when I outlined my fears to him that he was involved in this dispute too. He was in fact only attending a pre-marital course with a priest and that was the height of his links to the Church.

The following morning I saw my GP, now SDLP deputy leader Dr Alasdair McDonnell, about a stomach bug and he raced me out of his surgery. He would usually stop for a casual chat and I thought something was up.

I was concerned that something was up with a fellow student at the final Chartered Accountancy exam course when I attended a class that evening.

I had a dream that night. I dreamt that I was falling backwards and as I fell backwards, the ground disappeared and I was falling through space. I woke up with sweat on my brow and on my t-shirt. I had had a nightmare for the first time in my life.

My boss gave me cause for concern the next day when he had mysterious telephone calls from a former Sinn Fein councillor who was building a nursing home.

Something was wrong. I couldn't pin it down to something tangible or specific, but the sum total of all the various parts of the potential plots did not seem to be coincidental. I realised the enormity of the plot were all the people I suspected, from a Catholic priest to an SDLP councillor and doctor, actually to be involved.

I tried to talk about it to another one of my housemates, Ian, and he could see no reason for me to be afraid. Then I recalled that I had had a woman who claimed to be in the IRA back in my digs the previous week. I deduced that they were "casing the joint" in advance of an attack on me. I panicked.

I rang the police but they became a source of my concerns too as the policeman didn't seem to ask the right questions. I barricaded myself into my bedroom for a couple of hours and, at the instigation of my father, who I had telephoned, the police came back again and took me to the station where I spent the night in the waiting area.

Next morning, I went home to Derry with my friend Brian, my sister, and my older brother, who had come up to get me. I then rang Mark Durkan, now SDLP leader and MP for Foyle, who worked for John Hume, then MP for Foyle.

Mark said he would check out a few things, mainly concerning the fact that I may have happened upon an IRA cell in Belfast, and get back to me.

I went out, feeling much safer, that night. I went to my friend Brian's home and we discussed the matter. He became a slight concern for me after the chat.

Da Vinci's bar filled up with a rough crowd, as I have already described earlier in this book. Brian told me that "they" were going to shoot me dead and I was elevated. I was delighted to be getting all this attention from the IRA, but I was determined that they would not do anything that night.

I was not so sure the next day.

Fr Clerkin, my parish priest, was called in order to see if there was any conspiracy. He was in and out of the house for several days, but eventually came out with the immortal words: "You plough your own furrow, John. Isn't that right?"

He was in touch with the IRA, so he may have sensed that there were words being spoken by them about me, but that I was not involved in any kind of conspiracy against them. However, he left me with the merest impression that there had been some kind of conspiracy against me.

I then suspected that my sister, Marie, was involved in the conspiracy because she had shared a student house in Belfast with a girl who supported Sinn Fein. Marie told me that she knew what "it" was and the implication was that all would be revealed soon. Yet it seemed that "it" was something good as my sister was quite jovial in relation to discussing the matter.

When I raised the matter of "it" with my parents there was a whole hullabaloo. So I began to suspect that my parents were not to be trusted either. My parents soon wanted me to see a doctor "just for us" and this increased my feeling that they could not be trusted.

They called a family friend and doctor, Dr McClean, despite my protests. Dr McClean wanted me to take a tablet, but I insisted that I was alright. But there was no convincing everybody else there. Dr McClean wanted me to go to see a specialist doctor, but I was dead against it.

Then the television began to "talk" to me. First it was Gay Byrne on a repeat showing of the Late Late Show on Monday on Channel Four. I thought that his guests could see me.

Then it was the Terry Wogan Show on BBC 1. Terry's guest, Robbie Coltrane, made a thumbs-up signal to me. I was again sure that his guests could see me.

Then Charles Bronson came on television comforting his real-life wife Jill Ireland who, I found out later, was dying of cancer at that time. It was an interesting coincidence.

RTE's Questions and Answers political programme was next and I was sure that the programme makers were trying to quiz me about the guests.

That night I felt electrical sensations in my pillows, my bed, my body, my clothes and my head. It was as if I had been rigged with electrical devices which would supply current when the moment came.

I thought it was the CIA who had been providing the conspiracy with all the "sophisticated technology". Due to the fact that my family were involved, I concluded that they could only be protecting one man, John Hume, the Nobel Peace Prize winner and SDLP leader.

My father called Fr Clerkin again because I had kicked open my parents' bedroom door and, fully naked, roared that it was "John Hume".

Fr Clerkin took me to Gransha hospital.

There, I began to suspect the doctors and nurses, and even a fellow patient, who felt that I wasn't ill. Coincidence after coincidence happened to make me feel at the very least a little alienated from what the doctors were saying.

There was a good natured quality to all this conspiring in case anyone is in any doubt. I was never very worried or harassed or intimidated by what was happening. I didn't feel ill either, but I knew that things were happening to me that simply could not be unless...

...Unless there was some group involved who were capable of providing the "technology" and the "know-how".

The coincidences on television continued and I was slowly coming to the conclusion that no organisation would have the intensity of interest in me that this implied. I slowly came to the conclusion that it was God.

In this vein, a patient asked me one morning, 'Well, John, which is it to be, St John of God or John the Baptist?' I thought it may have been a message coming through him as the man was quite remote from our reality, but in touch with his own reality.

'Maybe I'm a prophet,' I told the doctor, thinking that the similarity between the word "profit", used heavily in accountancy, and the word "prophet" was meant to mean that I was being chosen because of my career.

I had lots of conspiracy theories, which in those early days in hospital I told to Fr Clerkin, who kindly came to see me at my request.

Then I felt that I had got to the bottom of Fr   Clerkin's reasons for seeing me and I stopped requesting that he make the journey to the hospital.

A nurse then became the focus for my questions for days on end as I tried to get to the bottom of the mysterious happenings that had brought me into hospital. But there didn't seem to be any explanation.

On the first weekend leave granted to me by the consultant I left the hospital and returned home. The bizarre coincidences had all but disappeared by then. That was why the consultant felt that I was returning to my health.

Of course, there was one massive coincidence that first evening of my freedom.

On Friday evening's news in early May, it was announced that Cardinal Tomás O'Fiaich, Roman Catholic Primate of All Ireland, had died suddenly on a pilgrimage to Lourdes. As the newsreader announced that he was aged 66, something jolted in my memory.

The memory of my experience in Galway, where I had worked out the name of Gerry Adams at 666 on my numeric alphabet, suddenly came back to me. The memory of the fact that Ian Paisley's name also came out at 666 returned too.

I waited for further details from the newsreader as I knew that it was likely that there was more to his death. He reported that Cardinal O'Fiaich had been born in November 1923 and was therefore exactly 66 years and 6 months old when he died, giving the coincidence of the three sixes (666). I was dumbfounded.

All my experiences had related to this 666 equation I had come across during the course of my life. I had somehow managed to forget about it, and yet I knew that I would not have forgotten about it unless God wanted me to forget about it. I was momentarily overwhelmed with fright, the last thing I needed if I was going to recover any time soon from my hospitalisation.

As I only thought the word "Antichrist", something jumped in my chest. I thought that I might be possessed, so I asked to see Fr Clerkin again.

My mother was against this as she felt that Fr Clerkin had spent enough time with me. Instead she and my father took me to Termonbacca Monastery and Retreat Centre, where a monk blessed me while I told him about the coincidences in relation to the late Cardinal and the two leading politicians. The monk seemed to show some restrained delight in hearing these things.

He told me not to try to fight evil or resist it as it was extremely powerful.

It was good advice. You cannot fight evil for you can only beat it by becoming even more evil, and that makes the world a worse place. You can only lead your own life in good faith, seeking to honour and serve God.

I reflected in the following weeks about the coincidence of Cardinal O'Fiaich's date of death. In those weeks, I was released completely from hospital, and my mind was allowed to wonder about matters.

I was pretty sure that I was not ill in the way that other people thought when I went into hospital. I know that I had been exhibiting the signs that I thought that people were involved in a conspiracy against me. But they had been giving me reasons to display those signs. That is my opinion to this date. But I have matured to some extent and I think that it was the angels speaking through them that persuaded me to believe momentarily that they hadn't my best interests at heart.

It was a case of being mugged by the same God who had allowed Jesus to have a beautiful experience of being teacher and healer, and then crucifixion victim.

I had been privileged to see these powers in action and yet it had effectively involved the ending of my career in accountancy.

Nonetheless, accountancy was now the least of my worries. I had seen the glory of the coming of the Lord and that was my primary worry. I really should not have worried then, but it had been a somewhat brutal, as well as beautiful, introduction to the powers of God. It certainly involved the God of Jesus.

I knew that I was special then. In those weeks after the end of my stay in hospital I became certain of something that had been occurring again and again during my time there. I became certain that I was being told that I was the Christ. I was the one who was awaited, the second coming of Christ.

I had no doubt about it. The experiences that I had been through left no room for doubt. I had effectively seen the angels in action and I had seen powers over human beings that only God was capable of having.

I had marks on my body too. I had the chicken pox marks on my forehead that looked as if they were healed crown of thorn marks; I had acne marks on my back that hinted that I had once leant against a cross; and I had a stretch mark in my abdomen which looked as if I had once been pierced with a sword.

However, the major reasons I came to the conclusion that I was the Christ involved having the powers of God exposed to me and having the number of the names of the two major bad guys from my political perspective, which was highly influenced by the ways of Jesus Christ, exposed to me as relevant and serious.

I had absolutely no doubt that I was Christ but I had grave reservations about being the Christ who everyone else thought was mentally ill.

I joked with my friends about being Christ and coming back to the hospital and taking the patients on a *One Flew over the Cuckoo's*

Nest bus run where I would heal them. However, I was to learn that I was not on a healing mission.

My job was to judge and, whatever anyone says, the best way to judge other people is to do it from below them in the pecking order of society. Rich people might then assume that I was jealous of their wealth just like most of the rest of the "peasants" but they would know that I had a point. It would have been evil to judge the world as the richest man because, not only would the judgement be hollow, it would also be born in really bad faith.

My job was a good faith engagement with humanity. I had come as the least of God's children to put the "shits" up the rich and powerful, who had failed to answer Jesus' invocation to us to do to the least of God's children as they would do to him. By just being "ill", I was in effect judging by Jesus' standards in a way that would be understood by the true faithful.

I always held the view that because my illness came about through God, it was something that could be healed. In the beginning I was to think that it didn't need any healing at all, that God would simply appear and tell everyone that I wasn't really ill, just chosen.

But as the months passed and more happened in relation to my "illness" it became apparent that God was giving me more and more reason to delve deeper into my undercover character as the concealed Christ.

80

Chapter Eight

God of the very ill

I went back to work in August 1990, and survived for a few days. I went home again, and tried to get back into work once again a couple of weeks later. This time I succeeded.

It was a strange time. The Omen and Damien films were on television and this interested me. I was also extremely interested in the comments of David Icke, the one-time soccer goalkeeper who had risen to become a broadcaster and leader of the Green Party in the UK. He told the world that he was the "Son of God". He also prophesied that twelve disasters would affect parts of the UK, including coincidentally Derry. His name, David, was also the name of my older brother, and even more mysteriously, his "surrogate" wife was called Marie, my sister's name, between whom I was born in our family.

I was amused at his honesty because it seemed to me at that time that the only thing you would get for being honest was ridicule. I myself had been very coy about telling anyone that I was the second coming of Christ because any time that I said it, I was made fun of. It was an impossible assertion, leaving you open to being called "mentally ill" because the only people who would usually call themselves a "Son of God" were the mentally ill.

Of course, I had a reason for being coy in the sense that any time I said that I was in any way special, people around me would become nervous that I was becoming ill again and often the way that they reacted to it was through humour spiked with anxiety.

'You're slipping,' a friend used to smile if he heard anything unusual from me. This was extremely bothersome as I was often aware that I was slipping to an extent. But that was in the sense that when I uttered any unusual words I was usually becoming disinhibited, and thus losing the fear of being criticised, rather than actually saying anything that I did not really believe all the time.

The difference between me and someone who was actually ill was that they would only say these things when they were ill and would not say them at any other time.

I had a meal with an angel, it seemed, just as I was about to become ill again. It seemed at times that God was with me in my illness, and that he was simply ensuring that I knew this by turning up in the midst of my symptoms and influencing each episode. By that reckoning I had to accept that I had an illness and God was standing by me, in a caring sort of way, and letting me know that he was overseeing things in order to ensure that they wouldn't get out of hand.

But the angel was special. She lived off the Ravenhill Road, linking her to Ian Paisley's largest Free Presbyterian church. I said strange things to her without reaction. The conversation was amazing, and punctuated with angelic special effects like a large wheel being rolled past our table for God knows what reason. I tried to tell her that I had "come to round the circle", or to do what had been done before. But the word "square" was thrust into my mind as I said the word "round" and my words sounded amusing.

But the angel never flinched. She was stunningly good-looking but I was becoming ill again as we spoke.

Eventually I ended up in Ballycastle and there I was totally in the hands of God. The seagulls passed over me threatening to offload on me, prompting me to rebuke God in my mind, because I knew that he was referring back to my seagull experience in Galway, whereupon the seagulls went away.

I was admitted to hospital again after driving around the city on the wrong side of the road and across the Foyle Bridge on the wrong side of the carriageway. The police rather decently only insisted that I go back into hospital.

I was released around six weeks later after "escaping" from the hospital and driving to Belfast, which resulted in me being put into a locked ward. I escaped from the locked ward too and went to Galway where I had a pleasant couple of days.

I was still sure that God was creating a lot of my experiences but I was coming to the conclusion that God wanted my illness to look as real as possible.

In the run-up to the third time I was admitted to hospital, my thoughts centred on a temptation experience that replicated one that Jesus had and a letter to the Derry Journal that seemed to have hidden meanings.

The temptation experience involved me being accompanied home after the bar one night in early February 1992. On the way, my companion, a solicitor, bid me to enter the grounds of my own parish church, St Patrick's, in order to waken up the parish priest for a conversation. I had told him that I knew who the Christ was and he wanted me to tell the priest. As it was late and we were both smelling of drink, I told him that it was not on.

Then he ordered me to climb up to the roof of the chapel. As soon as I heard him say "the roof", I knew what was happening.

'I suppose that you'll be telling me next to jump off the roof,' I mocked him.

'Yes, that's right. Jump off the roof!' he shouted. I ran off, knowing that Satan was speaking through him. But I was not afraid.

The letter was remarkable in that it contained so many Jesuitical references to politics in the North. Among other things, I made the remark that "it was checkmate for peace over violence" and this could have been construed as meaning that I, the prince of peace, had my adversary, the violence king, in check in the Chess sense so that he was beaten. That could also have been construed as the first public reference to my discovery in Galway as the reason I had Gerry Adams in check was because he had been exposed as the Antichrist. The argument that I was presenting was that there was no longer any basis for using violence in the conflict.

I had a powerful hallucination on the day I was admitted to hospital. I saw the face of John Major, the then British Prime Minister, protrude from the priest's face as he said a funeral mass for a distant relative. Then I cruised through the town, saying prayers with my mother in a little chapel and visiting the father of my assailant.

I had a fourth episode in April 1993. It was a severe psychosis lasting for several days. I was very ill. It really hit me then that I was suffering from a severe illness, or at least that God had given me a severe illness to deal with.

I was found naked and lying at the side of a road in county Galway, covered in scrapes as if I had had a fight with a lion. I had actually crawled naked through a thorn bush.

I had a belief that I was escaping from the imprisoned world, where my people were held, into the real world as I stripped off my clothes and ran naked through a field to reach the main road. The real world was where people had different clothes and was probably symbolic of the future.

I was taken to Ballinasloe Hospital for my troubles, where I stayed for a day and a night, and then on to Derry. Ballinasloe was 'no place to go'. It was like an old workhouse, where the patients sat at both sides of a great hall looking at each other.

In Gransha Hospital, I was in more familiar surrounds. Yet they had changed the locked ward to a new Intensive Care Unit (ICU) where five or six patients were kept, and the chronic patients were kept on another ward. It was a revelation.

It took me about a week to get back to normal during this admission. After that, I waited a couple of weeks before being released. I was diagnosed as manic-depressive at the end of my stay by Dr Artie O'Hara, a relatively decent doctor in terms of his treatment of me. It was welcome news. I was glad that they had not gone down the route of seeing me as schizophrenic, as it had a bad press.

Manic-depressives are just as likely to do stupid things but the press hasn't latched onto it yet. We are regarded as more gifted, more productive at times, and more creative. But it all depended on our mood swings, from our highs to our depressions.

I liked the ICU even though it was a locked ward. It had potential. When you were particularly ill, you needed the peace and quiet of the ICU in order to get back on your feet.

My fifth episode soon arrived in April 1994. It involved a sign from beyond when a St Brigid's cross on my bedroom wall moved mysteriously some distance down the wall. So I drove 'down' to mass, and then 'down' the country.

I arrived in Knock, county Mayo, at the shrine to Our Lady a few hours later. It was a funny trip when I saw the west of Ireland become very futuristic looking, as if oil had been discovered there and had made it very prosperous.

I drove to Letterkenny next, made a quiet scene in a Dunnes Stores shop by drinking mineral water without paying for it, and then headed back to Derry.

I had the funniest moment of my life in Da Vinci's bar, where I went on arriving in Derry. I hypnotized a businessman to believe that a radio presenter he really disliked with a passion had appeared in front of him.

'You're a bastard! You're a bastard! ... A f**king bastard!' he roared on 'seeing' the radio presenter. I didn't know what I had done at first to deserve this outburst.

I was almost a foot taller than this businessman and considerably broader, and so when he realized he was still standing in front of me, he went awfully quiet. Later, when I thought about it, I realized that I had hypnotized this man with a combination of my illness-oriented elation and the ensuing hypnotic charm.

Afterwards I went to a disco, and then to the Rising Sun, a county Derry bar where seven people had been shot dead the previous Halloween.

I then drove to Omagh where I attempted to book into a hotel. I had a row in the hotel bar with a loyalist paramilitary type. I unleashed a tirade of abuse at him and all he stood for as my tongue went wild with excitement.

I told him that I was the leader of the IRA, and that the IRA had buried their semtex, disguised as plasterboard, into the walls of major buildings in London.

He grabbed a bottle and thought for a moment about landing it on my face. I saw him, and moved my hand onto a glass as a deterrent. He pulled back. Then his friend pulled him back.

85

Ten minutes later I was sitting in my car in a ditch as it had slid off the road on black ice. I went to the nearest house, a few yards away. The next nearest was miles away. I was fortunate.

There was a bell outside the house, a very large bell for such an ordinary size house. I thought that it was the doomsday bell and that the world was about to end. It was so surreal.

An ambulance took me via casualty to the Tyrone and Fermanagh psychiatric hospital. I got out about two weeks later. I felt absolutely ravaged by the high that I had had, and the coming down to earth through the medication.

My sixth episode came a little earlier in the calendar year in late January 1995. I went on a trip around the northern half of county Donegal before deciding that I was becoming unwell. I sat in the house until a doctor came and admitted me to hospital.

It was relatively uneventful period of two weeks in hospital. The only strong memories I have are of an admirable old woman and a young woman I grew to like. The old woman, who was both deaf and dumb, was admitted with some depression too, and she used to throw things about the room in frustration. I felt for the young woman because she was affected by her illness from so young an age and she was a very good-natured person who recognized me as a good person. This was important for me because I felt that she would know.

In April 1995, my brother Conal, a Chartered Accountant, was married to Valerie, his girlfriend of years. My sister had also got married the previous January to Jorgos, a Greek she had met while working as an English teacher in a small town near Athens.

The combination of these weddings made me feel so utterly lonely that I was losing family members younger than me, and who seemed happy in their lives whereas I was not. I felt that the time had come when I should meet someone who could make me feel happy in all of the turmoil of my life.

I asked God to intervene as I approached my seventh admission to hospital. I wanted him to provide me with someone who would love me and who I could love in turn.

I also explicitly expressed for the first time my belief that my "numbers" equation was the real thing. I prepared a simple sheet with the numeric alphabet on it with numbers beside each letter. I then typed that "Ian Paisley" equals "Gerry Adams", which equals 666. I sent the sheet to army bases and to Protestant Churches, mainly Free Presbyterian churches and ones who competed with them for members. Somehow this was going to create problems for Ian Paisley.

Yet Paisley seemed to me to be aware of my "numbers" equation because he reacted very strongly when the talks chairman of that time, Senator George Mitchell, referred to "the twin demons of Northern Ireland, violence and intransigence". The reference to him as a "demon" was too much for Paisley and he demanded Mitchell's resignation.

On the day of the admission I was aggressive for the first time, the frustration of another episode beckoning getting to me. I grabbed my Greek brother-in-law by the throat after he was cheeky to me on the telephone and I scared the wits out of a doctor who came out to my home to admit me, intimidating him in a fierce manner.

When I got to the hospital, I found that there was a doctor there who fitted the bill as my partner. She was very attractive, and very good-natured. She was like the girl next door, but she was also someone who attracted me with her sense of love. She somehow demanded that I love her when she treated me and I responded to this.

I was on track to be released fairly quickly but the young doctor entered the living room of the ICU during a quiz and I felt that I impressed her by answering a couple of questions. I felt very good. I asked a fellow patient for a cigarette and I smoked it. I told a nurse that I only smoked when I was getting high. She told the doctor and I was refused leave I had already been granted. I was furious. I ordered forty cigarettes and began a severe smoking habit that practically bankrupted me for several years.

Five weeks later I got out on leave and became ill again. The attractive doctor, out of inexperience, didn't notice that I was ill until I practically told her myself towards the end of the week after my leave.

I was aggressive again as I grabbed the consultant over a table while he readied himself to go home for the weekend. I was adamant that he should release me. All I got for my troubles was a transfer back to the ICU.

There, the young doctor and I had arguments over whether genes can be patented, after we continued with a discussion I had raised during my week of illness. She was ill-advised to partake of the discussion unless she actually wanted a relationship with me. But you know what doctors are like. They can't resist the temptation to always be right, even when they're wrong. She was wrong. Attempts were being made to patent genes.

I was finally released after eleven weeks when the doctors were made aware that I was not smoking because I was ill and because I told them that I always believed that there was significance to the 666 names, and not just when I was ill.

The nurses in the ICU proved to be false friends in this respect as they were the ones who were poisoning the consultant against my release.

I loved the attractive young doctor now and it seemed that she might just be the one to break the rules of her profession. She had certainly broken every other rule of her profession in her dealings with me.

After being released from hospital I undertook quite a few undercover operations to try to check out the young doctor, and was almost caught "stalking" her. I was innocently going about my observations, but the prejudice of the medical profession almost labelled me a "stalker". I was sinking into depression in the midst of this and was thinking of ending it all because the pain was so severe. I was very annoyed especially by the thought that I had been caught by the doctor I loved trying to observe her.

I then went into what is termed "rapid-cycling" or having four episodes in the same year. However, I managed to abort most of those episodes. I nipped the symptoms in the bud several times – in

April, July and September 1996 – by a process of observation and early intervention, and I prevented myself from going into hospital.

In July, I had gone to mass in the aftermath of a killing in the city by the British army and the priest asked very relevantly, 'What would Jesus do? Jesus teaches forgiveness…' As he said the word "forgiveness", there was a loud bang in the Church beside me, where a kneeling rest was disturbed, and I felt the presence of the angels.

In September I went to a healing mass before aborting the episode. It stimulated my sense of being Christ and helped to provoke the episode.

In January 1997, I had another aborted episode. This time it went so smoothly, after I had caught the symptoms so early, that I was lulled into a false sense of security. I felt that it would always be like this from then on.

It was not, as I found out in April. The symptoms persisted and were riding the wave provided by the medication. I couldn't sleep and instead ended up ringing my GP several times. I also rang my former beloved doctor and my parish priest, Fr Clerkin. I tried to stay out of hospital for another day by travelling to my uncle's home in county Donegal but then voluntarily admitted myself to hospital after almost falling asleep at the wheel which scared the wits out of me.

In June 1997 two things happened almost concurrently. The first was that I was tested for *sleep apnoea* and, finding that I needed it, was fitted for a mask to wear in bed attached to a continuous pressured air pump (CPAP). It has helped me to get a good night's sleep and taken away most of the tiredness that had afflicted me.

The second was a dispute in our park with some of the neighbours complaining that things needed to be done. My father was central to this dispute, and was insulted on Radio Foyle by one of the protagonists. I took grave exception to this and, as I was becoming ill, managed to respond to the insult by making life uncomfortable for the man one night.

We discussed the Book of Revelation on admission to hospital, and the other patients seemed to know quite a lot. One eventually asked, 'What about the Ten Virgins?'

I thought that this was still the Book of Revelation and I couldn't recall the answer. But I found out the answer when I returned home and found my Bible lying open at Matthew Chapter 24. The *Parable of the Ten Virgins* was there on the open pages and it was quite a coincidence that my bible was lying open at that page.

After this episode I was advised in September 1997 to go on a small dose of anti-psychotic medication and this medication has transformed my life by preventing all subsequent hospitalisations to this date with the exception of one that I go on to describe.

But God was never very far away, as the *Parable of the Ten Virgins* may show. I was biding my time until God would open up with me. In the meantime I believed that God's plan for me was to see what life was like for the mentally ill, including the tragedies and the rejections they face.

Chapter Nine

God of the Irish

My very attractive beloved doctor, whose first name was Paddy, was on my mind quite a lot from when I first met her in August 1995. In Autumn 1997 I spent seven weeks, immediately after going on the new drug, preparing what amounted to a proposal of marriage. I had found out some things about her, which I included in the detailed proposal, and I believed that she was the bride of Christ as prophesied in the Book of Revelation (Rev 19:7-8).

Paddy's full Christian name, Patricia, was significant as she was being chosen because she was representative of Ireland, as the twelve apostles were representative of the twelve tribes of Israel. I was after all the Irish Christ, and I was choosing an Irish bride.

Patricia was symbolic of Ireland as it was the female version of Patrick, the patron saint. The female gender of the name and of Paddy was important, because Ireland was symbolised in history as *Mother Ireland*.

It was the perfect name for the bride of the Irish Christ. It was a beautiful name, and Paddy was a beautiful woman. Ireland was a beautiful country and I was to marry *Mother Ireland*.

Another coincidence that occurred to me was that both my surname and Paddy's originated in the county of Kerry, in the southwest corner of Ireland. I had known this for some time, but I had not drawn any conclusion. It was also quite a coincidence.

It occurred to me too that the county of Kerry was also referred to as *the Kingdom county*. It was often referred to simply as *the Kingdom*. Kerry was *the Kingdom*. This was interesting. Both Paddy and I were the bearers of surnames that were from *the Kingdom*.

It was a fitting place for the Christ and his bride to come from. But since we had come from outside *the Kingdom*, it was appropriate that we had names that had their origins in *the Kingdom*.

Kerry was therefore symbolically *the Kingdom of God*, and the Christ and his bride were to be symbolically from this Kingdom. Moreover, they were to be immersed in the beautiful mythology of Ireland, particularly of the west of Ireland.

In the proposal I told Paddy that it was difficult to think of a good reason why I was going through what I was going through. I knew it was God's will, and I believed that in a literal sense.

I thought that there was a chance that I was the great auditor from heaven, who was checking the way that the least of God's children were being treated. I was thirsty and you gave me to drink. I was naked and you clothed me. I was in prison and you came to visit me. It had all happened. Thirsty, I had called at the door of a stranger and he had given me cups of water. I was found naked by a roadside, and clothed. I was in the ICU, a prison, and people had visited me.

So in a sense I knew that I was the Christ while compiling my proposal. I had absolutely no doubt about it. God was guiding me as a person to the conclusion that I was his chosen one. I had only to look at where I lived and I found some intriguing coincidences.

Derry was the New Jerusalem so far as I was concerned. It had the walled inner city, the most complete set of walls in Europe, and these walls were symbolic of the New Jerusalem's walls in the Book of Revelation.

Indeed the old Jerusalem had its walls, which the Romans had destroyed only to find that a new empire, based in a different part of the world and in a different era, had built another beautiful fortress where the Lamb was to reside.

Derry, the place of so much oppression over the last several hundred years, was the place where the 144,000 citizens, who had the name of the Lamb and his father written on their foreheads, were to reside.

> Then I looked and there before me was the Lamb, standing on Mount Zion, and with him 144,000 who had his name and his father's name written on their foreheads. (Rev 14:1)

Thus the Lamb was to have a name, and his father was to have a name, and in human terms this name would be significant for the 144,000 who lived in the New Jerusalem.

I interpreted the phrase 'written on their foreheads' in a creative manner. To me, it meant that the name was to be so obvious that no-one could miss it. My name held special significance now that I realised that names were all-important.

I had the most famous surname in the history of Ireland, O'Connell, due to the efforts of the Liberator of Irish Catholics, Daniel O'Connell, and it was fitting that my name, the name of the Irish Christ, was to be so. It was the most powerful name in the Irish historical sense, immersing the Irish Christ into the midst of Irish history and culture even further.

But the Liberator had a son called John O'Connell, and so in a sense I was the son of the Liberator, another way of saying the Son of God, the ultimate liberator.

But my name was even more important in the context of Derry, the New Jerusalem. The walled city of Derry was situated in a peninsula called Inishowen, or in English, the island, as it formerly was, of John. So I lived on the island of John.

But the peninsula was situated in the ancient kingdom of Tyrconnell, meaning in Irish, 'the land of Connell'. So I also lived in the land of Connell.

I was John O'Connell, John of the clan Connell, living on 'the island of John in the land of Connell', my name and my father's name 'written on their foreheads' (Rev 14:1), or so obvious it couldn't be missed. It was a monumental coincidence. I was the Lamb of God. I had no doubt about that.

There was also the saint and founder of Derry, who made prophecies about Derry.

The king who will cause a lasting change,

Shall be from Desmond – the prediction is correct –
Goodness forever after that time.

(From The Prophesies of St Malachy and St Colmbkille by Peter Bander
(Colin Smythe Gerrards Cross))

Colmcille predicted that a king from Desmond would come to cause 'a lasting change'. He emphasises that the prophecy is correct when he refers to the man from Desmond.

There shall be 'goodness forever after that time'. Colmcille is undoubtedly referring to the second coming of Christ when he refers to the man from Desmond.

Desmond was a kingdom in the times of Colmcille, roughly centred around county Kerry. Although I am not from county Kerry, my surname is. On top of this fact, my middle name is Desmond. My full name, therefore, John Desmond O'Connell, is significant in that it takes account of both the prophecies of the Book of Revelation and the prophecies of the founding saint of Derry, Colmcille.

My proposal also included articles from various religious, political and sociological writers copied from magazines, including mention of liberation theology, the concept of More and a chapter about Christina Gallagher, the county Mayo stigmata sufferer and visionary, copied from a book I had got from a friend of my mother.

I also included an early draft of a chapter from a book I was then writing which had made reference to one of my temptations, where the devil – in the form of a solicitor – had bid me to jump from the roof of Pennyburn chapel. I didn't include this reference in the final book as I didn't want to make anything of the fact that I believed that I was Christ. I didn't think that too many people would believe me because of the illness.

All in all it was a beautiful proposal to Paddy. But I didn't send it at that time. I asked for my parish priest to help me in taking it to Paddy but he was reluctant because he sensed that I might be "stalking" Paddy, and so I decided that then was not the right time to send it.

94

So I let it sit for a couple of years bar a few letters to Paddy explaining what I had intended to tell her in the proposal.

In September 1999, I began a temporary clerical job with Derry Roads Service, a Civil Service job, and it was fairly easy work. But there were more traumas ahead.

The experience of SDLP leader Mark Durkan's niece in January 2000 really scared me as she had effectively foreseen her own death. She saw herself in a dream looking up out of a coffin and this eighteen-year-old ran to her parents in a fright. She died the next day in a road accident. SDLP MP Eddie McGrady's niece also died in a vicious sexually-motivated attack at about the same time, and I thought it was no coincidence.

There was a blackness entering my life that meant that the year, 2,000 A.D., when most of the prophecies about Christ's coming signaled that there would only be good things, including the public declaration that there was a Christ, was going to be very bad for me.

My book came out at this time too, and was selling quite slowly. In March, I was tense about the book and about the fact that my job was to finish.

The angels, who would communicate with me occasionally, usually through coincidences, suggested that Paddy had moved house to a new address I had found. The address had been in a medical book in the library and I found it by accident.

I went to deliver a book there in late March, but she wasn't there and her letter box was too small for it. This was to prove very unfortunate for me.

On April 1st I was given a message by the local IRA because my book had mentioned the 666 of Gerry Adams. The message seemed to be in the form of an April Fool tinged with a threat that they would get me even if it meant using a discredited republican who would not lead the police or the public back to Sinn Fein.

It was not all bad. Later in April, Gerry Adams spoke in Derry at the annual Easter Rising commemoration. The weather turned bad on the poor republicans and they were faced with a mixture of lightning, thunder, rain, large drops of hail, and summer heat. The local newspaper described how Gerry Adams spoke amid thunder and lightning in the city's cemetery. I was very amused at this as he was like Dracula in his castle surrounded by thunder and lightning.

Paddy sent a letter I wrote to her back to my doctor, trying to suggest that I was ill. My doctor asked to see me but, on seeing me, concluded that I wasn't ill.

A few weeks later I sent Paddy another letter. It was slightly angry as I was becoming a little disinhibited and frustrated after my experiences with the book, the job, the deaths of SDLP representatives' nieces, the April Fool as well as her returning my letter.

The tone of the letter was cheeky and forward in a way that I hadn't been with Paddy before. As I was going to Belfast that Thursday I decided to take the letter with me. However, I got a sign as I left for Belfast and decided to also take a pen and writing paper with me. When I got there I wrote a much more humble letter to Paddy, who I thought the sign was suggesting was tired and not sleeping because of my actions. In my sign I had actually seen a woman in a shop wearing a name badge with "Patricia" on it and she looked very tired. It was a coincidence.

When I arrived in Belfast, I wrote Paddy a soft letter apologizing and telling her that I wished it wasn't so and that all I wanted was her love.

I posted the letter instead of going to Paddy's home and I put the book which had enclosed with it the original angry letter in the post too in Belfast because I suspected that the post was being scrutinized in Derry and was thus not getting through. Nonetheless, I knew she would be outraged by the two letters and the book arriving simultaneously.

Next day Paddy called the police. They arrived with me telling me that "a nurse" had called them. She was not pressing charges but she could do if I persisted. It seems that God hadn't told Paddy that she was the bride of Christ.

Paddy's retaliation in calling the police proved troublesome. I was increasingly exhausted and making mistakes. I was finished with writing letters to Paddy but I wrote other letters that allowed a cowardly thug, for the second time in my life, to assault me.

This cowardly thug was my consultant who, six weeks after the police called, suddenly took an interest in my case. I had stimulated her interest by asking for a meeting, which lasted two hours, and in which I got angry with her because she had said that I might be becoming ill. I then wrote a letter to her which she suggests confirmed to her that I was "ill" and thinking of suicide. I had actually simply declared that I was Christ, not "ill", as she interpreted it. She denies I had ever told her that I was Christ even though it was in my book, which she read so thoroughly she was trying to promote it with the drug reps. In relation to the suicide threat, I had not made any, only an oblique reference to feeling an attraction to the spirit world.

Bad faith motivated my consultant when she made moves to have me brought into hospital. But I had left her room to maneuver by writing the letter, which was simply an attempt to send an apology to Paddy through her. My GP contributed to this ignorance by trying to blackmail me into hospital. I really should have drove to Galway at that point and avoided the hospitalization.

A young doctor at the hospital felt that I was not ill, and checked to see if I could go home with her consultant. He said that I should stay to see my consultant.

I had simply treaded on the sensibilities of the consultant and her huge, ugly ego and she had responded, first by ensuring that she had enough to get me on, and then by asserting her power over me. It was assault, but somehow she felt, like the previous person who had assaulted me, that she would get away with it.

The previous time I was assaulted it was because of my beliefs in the SDLP or the Christian way. This time it was because I believed that I was the Christ, which I had every reason to believe. Both times I was assaulted by people with great ugliness in their hearts, and the state protected them on both occasions. But God will not.

I only have to stand back and observe as their lives are affected by the God they both probably go to church on Sunday to worship. But God hates a hypocrite, and I can smile at what God has done to them. Of course, I cannot respond myself, and both these ugly characters knew that, because that would be "an eye for an eye" and I am against that. But God has his own justice.

I sent another letter to the consultant before I went into hospital. I wasn't taking it lying down. When she received this letter, she told me in a meeting that she was referring me to a forensic psychiatrist because of my references to Paddy. I was going to have to stay in hospital until the forensic psychiatrist saw me and my letters.

A feeling on my head of anxiety appeared that night. It was to be the subject of a miraculous cure later in my life in Medjugorje, so I am led to believe that it was meant to happen and that my battle with the consultant was also meant to happen.

At first it was just a fleeting feeling that lasted a few moments and then went completely away. It then recurred after about an hour and then went away again. Next day it got slightly worse. It would last longer when it came and would come back sooner.

Nonetheless, it seemed that the feeling did not relate to anything that I was consciously feeling and it was almost comical in its disposition. I sensed, in fact, that the feeling itself was coming from God and I felt that it was his way of saying that I had to suffer for a while. Whatever it was, it was never that real at the start.

But it became very real after a while. I felt that my life was over and that God was indicating that I should leave this cruel world that seemed to only ever back the evil and corrupt people. I was sure that the best way to punish the world for its lack of faith in God was to end my life.

But I had one communication from God before I left the hospital. On the day that the forensic psychiatrist looked at my letters at my local clinic my heart flamed up into a blaze that lasted for hours and I had what I would term *a religious experience*. It was a sign that I had the sacred heart, the pure heart that had been purified, and that God would always protect me. In my own mind I was back in the good books of God. The forensic psychiatrist thought that I should be released from hospital straight away because the letters were not a risk.

He saw me a few weeks later but, at a second meeting, decided that he didn't need to see me any further after I had wisely told him of my SDLP connections, and had threatened nurses that I was going to sue him.

However, I spent the summer thinking of ways to kill myself as I went into a depression, a depression added to by the forensic psychiatrist's desire to see me again. He had told me that he needed to see me until Christmas, but when it came to our second meeting in October he had somehow decided that he had only ever needed to see me again in order to close off the case. He was such a coward and a liar. The fact was that I was sending out signals that I was going to sue. I don't know how much the SDLP connections affected him but the combination of lawsuit and political connections possibly meant to him that I wouldn't be ignored.

In August, we went on holiday to a cottage beside the Drowse River in county Leitrim, near Bundoran, and this lifted my mood and made me see that my life was just about worth saving. I had thoughts of suicide when I returned home but never as intensely.

However, I threw a rope around a branch of the tree at the bottom of our garden and thought earnestly about killing myself. But my sister and her young children were due back from Greece that afternoon and the thought that they would arrive with my parents and find me hanging on the tree put me off doing it.

So a combination of a two week holiday and a little bit of good fortune at the right time helped me to survive the symptoms of depression until the effects of an anti-depressant kicked in. But it was the most traumatic period in my life.

I did make a formal complaint against my consultant and this resulted in her being investigated by the Northern Ireland Ombudsman, who took her to task for not keeping proper records of her meeting with the forensic psychiatrist, of the referral to him, and the Ombudsman took him to task for not presenting a report. No-one knew then what grounds she had really been using in her attempt, as she was dishonestly to imply, at helping a colleague, or Paddy. She was simply assaulting me because I had injured her

99

huge ugly ego, and in my opinion she had no thoughts of helping Paddy at all.

But God was with me and just because I can't reply to these people doesn't mean that he won't. The living God has replied and will always reply. In that sense he was to reply to my plea to bring an end to the world that bolsters up people who would assault other people including my former consultant and my lawyer assailant. I believe that process began in September 2001.

It was my thirty-sixth birthday on September 10th 2001. That night I went to a musical together with my cousin on the first night of performances at the new Millennium Forum theatre. The show, 'Rent', was based in New York at the time of rent strikes, and was basically a condemnation of American capitalism.

The very next day the world changed forever. New York was attacked and the World Trade Center collapsed after two fully-occupied aircraft were slammed into its towers. Over 3,000 people were said to have tragically perished.

There are links with the Book of Revelation in the New York attack. 'New York' as a name comes out at 666 on my numeric alphabet, on which Gerry Adams and Ian Paisley's names come out at 666.

For months, I contemplated the possibility that New York is the 'great city', Babylon, of the Book of Revelation.

> "'Woe! Woe, O great city,
> O Babylon, city of power!
> In one hour your doom has come!'"   (Rev 18:10)

In one hour, on Tuesday 11th September 2001, New York was brought to its knees.

Oddly enough, the beard became an issue in its aftermath in Afghanistan where the Taliban leaders, and Osama Bin Laden sympathisers, insisted on men growing beards. I had been trying to grow a beard for a couple of months at that stage, but it was never thick enough – too many female hormones – and I had to make do with a goatee.

In a strange and subconscious sense therefore, I was both in Afghanistan in the weeks before the attack and in New York on the night before the disaster due to my beard and the 'Rent' show respectively. In January 2002, I came to the conclusion that this choreography of my activities was inspired, and that this was indeed a message from the angels. September 11th is therefore significant in my mind as the fulfillment of a Book of Revelation prophecy.

The great empire, Babylon, whose origin is in the actions of Adam, the founder of all empires, has fallen. All empires have fallen by extension of the logic of Adam's fall, the fall of man, and God is guiding us to safety. God, through the militant Islamists, was destroying the perception of absolute invulnerability and power that the United States' empire had projected by putting a hole in its side below the waterline. The United States was going to struggle now to achieve its potential as an empire. In reality, its claim to be a great power had been severely dented. And I knew that we had begun the process of ending the terrorist hegemony of capitalism and imperialism that dominated the value systems of the two thugs who had assaulted me.

Yet it wasn't for me that I was involved in all this. I could take the knocks, even if it was only just at times. But others could not. These people, and people like them with their huge ugly egos had left a trail of people who had fallen victim to them. And the world protected them because they made lots of money. And the little people suffered.

The world was going to change for the little people. Of that I was sure.

.

101

Chapter Ten

Miraculous healing?

I wrote six other books in the period from September 2001 to the date of my first trip to Medjugorje in August 2006.

The first I wrote, called *Love is the Answer: The SDLP, Christianity and the Northern Ireland Conflict,* dealt specifically with my "numbers" experience in Galway and what I had been given over the years by God by way of analysis of the equation. It was undoubtedly the most important book that I had ever written, not because it mentioned the numbers, but because it contained insights into the way that God thought about the two beasts and their influence on the world. It was framed in a way that accentuated the good attributes of the SDLP and social democracy generally, but it was mainly a vehicle I used to heighten awareness of the two beasts. I got good newspaper and radio coverage but it didn't particularly sell well; however, it performed its task quite well.

I wrote two novels then, *The Calling of Sinead*, about a woman being called to politics, and *The Hunger File*, about a young accountant facing a traumatic tax investigation of hunger strike monies owned by the IRA mob. I then wrote *Heavenly Bliss!* about my rather blunt forgiveness of my lawyer assailant, and *The Bride of Christ* about my experiences with Paddy.

My seventh book was entitled *My Life in the Eden Zone* and it describes my life in a paradise of sorts, which my life has been except for a couple of notable periods when nothing would have convinced me that I was special.

As my second trip to Medjugorje beckoned, I was not really getting too overwhelmed. I was pretty annoyed by the feeling of anxiety in my head, and it was even worse now that I could compare it to the normal feeling after my healing the previous August. But I had learned to deal with it and was coping well despite the frustration and the nuisance value of it.

There was just one announcement in the Parish Bulletin in March to advertise the trip to Medjugorje. The price was the same as the previous year, £399 plus £70 for a single room, but the trip had the added advantage that it was flying out of the City of Derry Airport. I was pretty sure that I would go on the trip, but I did not ring Adele's number straight away.

There was a little part of my mind that doubted that I would get any healing out of the trip and so I was slow to move. A couple of weeks later I decided that I would ring the number the following Monday or Tuesday.

But as it turned out Adele rang me on the Sunday to ask me if I had heard that they were flying out of the City of Derry Airport. I told her I had and that I was just about to ring her, and she was amazed at the coincidence.

It *was* quite a coincidence and it was a coincidence that began the build up to my second journey to the Bosnian village. I got a brochure from Adele and made the reservation for a week from the 7th to the 14th June.

There was something about the date that interested me. Seven is an important number to God in the Bible and this appealed to me. Also, the fact that June was the sixth month meant that the date of our journey there was the seventh day of the sixth month of the seventh year of the new millennium. There was something strangely appealing in the number of man, or six, being mixed in with the number of God, or seven. It seemed like a good day to travel.

So I was beginning to look forward to my trip to Bosnia. It seemed that it was going to be an interesting trip.

I had told Adele that I was going to thank Our Lady for the healing she had given me the previous summer. I didn't want to go into the fact that the healing had been withdrawn and that part of my reason for going was to receive some more healing. I didn't want her to think that I was ungrateful to Our Lady for interceding on my behalf in the first place, or that I was a bad person for having lost the healing that I had been given.

But people who've been to Medjugorje will know that there is an element of calling to the place. Our Lady calls and we answer the call. I felt this call especially the first time around even though I wasn't sure whether it was Lourdes or Fatima or Medjugorje I was being called to. Nonetheless, when I decided to go to Medjugorje it seemed to really open up a channel that called much more intensely until I got there.

Spring 2007 was an interesting time politically in the North of Ireland and in Britain. The St Andrews Agreement a few months previously had heralded a return to Stormont rule in the North with Ian Paisley and Gerry Adams leading the way. In fact, Martin McGuinness took over as Paisley's deputy with Adams playing an informal presidential role overseeing both men in their running of the North.

I was relieved that I finally had Paisley and Adams in the position of power that I needed them to be in in order to fulfill some of the more opaque prophecies of the Book of Revelation. Several prophecies were fulfilled in the period, and I sent details to SDLP MLAs and to the press.

In the run up to the elections, Adams "hijacked" Clonard monastery for a political meeting.

> "[The man of lawlessness or the Antichrist] will oppose and will exalt himself over everything that is called God or is worshipped, so that he sets himself up in God's temple, proclaiming himself to be God." (2 Thes 2:3-4)

He was of course "proclaiming himself to be God" in a logical sense when he believes that armed struggle is superior to the Christian nonviolent way of our God and, refusing to repent of that view, sets himself up in God's temple.

I sent Paisley and Adams a copy of *Love is the Answer* as soon as they were set up in Stormont as the leaders of the largest parties, and asked them to repent before going into government. It was a symbolic effort designed to get these *egomaniacal* men to recognize their *own* evil, and to mark the occasion on which I had revealed myself as Christ to them.

Another prophecy was fulfilled by the fact that Adams remained outside government on the reconvening of Stormont on May 8th:

> "[The second beast, i.e. Paisley] exercised all the authority of the first beast [i.e. Adams] on his behalf [i.e. because Adams remained outside government], and made the earth and its inhabitants worship the first beast, whose fatal wound had been healed [Adams was shot and seriously wounded in 1984]" (Rev 13:12).

It was a time of much significance and I felt that I was nearing the point where all would be revealed and my supposed journey into *Never Never Land* would be recognised as valid and divine in origin.

But there was much more to it than the simple coincidences relating to the North. The British prime minister, Tony Blair, announced that he was retiring and this allowed me to work out a final part of Revelation's jigsaw puzzle. I found out that Gordon Brown was not going to last long as Prime Minister. But first Adams would play up.

I think that the prophecies point to an unpleasant good-bye gift from Adams and Paisley. That may mean some violence. This comes from the verse, "he [i.e. the Antichrist] once was, now is not, and yet will come" (Rev 17:8).

The Antichrist who "once was, now is not" is a reference to the fact that Adams was acting once as the Antichrist (i.e. during the Troubles) and "now" is no longer acting in that way. "Yet will come" indicates that before the prophecies will end, he will return to being the Antichrist. This was always going to happen as no-one insisted on Adams repenting of his past. But the question is, when will the prophecies end?

Interpreting the next verses gives a timescale for the fulfilment of the prophecies. "The seven heads are seven hills on which the woman sits. They are also seven kings," (Rev 17:9). The seven hills symbolise Rome, built on seven hills, so the author of Revelation is attacking the Roman Empire. But the comparable empire in our context and era is the British Empire and the city comparable to Rome is London. So the seven kings come from London.

Those kings are described as: "Five have fallen, one is, and the other has not yet come" (Rev 17:10). Coincidentally during the Troubles, the Troubles being the key timeframe, five London Prime Ministers have fallen: Wilson, Heath, Callaghan, Thatcher, and Major. "One is," or the sixth Prime Minister, must refer to Tony Blair under whom much of the changes to the North took place. The other who has not yet come is remarked: "…but when he does come he must remain for a little while" (Rev 17:10). I think that this must refer to Gordon Brown who won't be Prime Minister for long by this account.

The fact that Blair is referred to as "one is" demonstrates that major prophecies have occurred under his rule while he "is", and also while the Antichrist "is not" (see above). But the whole sequence of verses, ante-ceded with the proviso, "This calls for a mind with wisdom," (Rev 17: 9), making them the most mysterious verses in the Book of Revelation, also signals that the whole framework will have outworked itself by the time of the seventh king, "who has not yet come, but when he does come he must remain for a little while".

So when Gordon Brown, the seventh king, stops being Prime Minister, which won't be long according to the prophecies, Ian Paisley and Gerry Adams will be disgraced and in turmoil, or "thrown alive into the fiery lake of burning sulphur" (Rev 19:20). The intriguing question is what happens under Gordon Brown that leads to this outcome.

I had unveiled the most difficult area of the Book of Revelation, and I had no doubt, nor do I have now, that I am correct in my interpretation of these sequences of events. For years I had sought answers to the above prophecies and simply could not work them out. Now I was getting places. It won't be long until all will be revealed.

Our flight was slightly delayed, but it went smoothly, and our bus journey to Medjugorje went as planned. So we arrived in Medjugorje late in the early hours of Friday morning. I got about three hours sleep that first night before we were up for breakfast and mass.

I wondered that morning about how long it would take for the trumpet to sound and for the angel of the Lord to touch my head again. But I reassured myself that I was going to have to be patient.

I went to confession that first evening as I had done the previous time. I was waiting a long time, but not as long as the previous time, in a queue for a priest to become available. Suddenly, a few priests arrived at the one time, and they each opened a little confession box.

So I went to one of the newly-arrived priests and I was his first punter of the evening. He was certainly fresh and ready for me when I went in. He was an American priest, a young man of, say, thirty-five to forty years old, slightly balding but with dark hair, tall and slim, and a sturdy build.

I told him straight away that I had come to Medjugorje for a healing because an anxiety feeling in my head that had been healed the previous year had come back. He was listening intently.

I hadn't really a lot of sins to tell, but I told him a few out of courtesy to him and his job as priest. I had told an old English-speaking Croatian priest the same sins the previous time and had recounted these sins many times before, years before when I had actually gone to confession, and simply gained absolution. But this time was different. I had caught a priest possibly fresh on the first night of his pilgrimage to Medjugorje and he was in a pretty elevated state.

He pulled me up about one sin in particular. He wanted me to do something about it. He suggested saying a prayer if I was thinking of sinning in that way. I was mortified that the priest had mentioned my misdemeanour. I said I would try my best.

Then he stood up and said that he was going to try some healing. He laid his hands on my head, another indication that he was elevated and fresh, but he was in the right area if he was going to effect a healing of my anxiety feeling. He stood there for what seemed like an eternity, praying over me silently.

I didn't know what was going to happen. The feeling would normally go away momentarily if someone laid their hands on my head. So I thanked the priest for his efforts after he finished his prayers, not knowing whether or not he had actually healed me in any way.

In fact I assumed that he hadn't even though the worst part of the anxiety feeling, the sensation at the top of my head, had gone completely. But I was tired and I was not thinking that clearly.

The next morning we climbed *Apparition Hill*, where the children visionaries had witnessed their first vision of Our Lady in 1981. We got up at around six o'clock in the morning to do this climb due to the heat in the afternoon. That night I told another pilgrim that all I had come for was the healing, so I suspect that I still had the feeling.

The following day we got up at five o'clock in the morning to climb *Cross Mountain* and it was exhilarating. I had shied away from climbing this mountain on my first trip because I didn't think that I would be able for it and so I was delighted to do it. I had done one of the things I set out to do on coming to the village for a second time.

The second thing I wanted to do on my first trip, but had not been able to, was to travel to the Croatian city of Dubrovnik. The next day we corrected this and my trip to Medjugorje was made. I was very happy but very tired.

Dubrovnik was an amazing tourist city and the scenery both there and on the taxi journey, which cost the four of us fifty Euros each, was absolutely stunning. I was amazed at the tourist product that this walled city had provided and drew parallels in my mind with what my own walled city of Derry could become if properly promoted. Perhaps they may even come to Derry as pilgrims.

I had only one stunning memory after that. Brendan, a Belfast pilgrim, suggested praying for a cure under the massive statue of Jesus at the back of St James' chapel, and I went there one afternoon. I said some prayers, touched the weeping knee of Jesus, where what are said to be human tears seem miraculously to flow from little cracks in the copper statue's right knee, and sat down. I could vaguely feel the anxiety feeling on the back of my head. Somehow I sensed that there was an evil involved in this sensation.

'I cast thee out, Satan,' I then said stridently.

The back of my head was almost torn away from the rest of my head, as if someone had just pulled my hair sharply, and I felt something go. That was the last time I was to feel anything there.

So the combination of the American priest's laying on of hands and my casting out of Satan seems to have done the job. There is still a light sensation around my ears but this is no trouble at all. I had got the cure that I wanted.

I didn't actually realise that I had been cured of the problem until after I had returned home. I was praying throughout my stay in the village for healing and it just didn't seem to me that I had been healed. Though right from the first night at confession I sensed that there had been an improvement.

I was often tired after nights of little sleep in the Bosnian heat, and I was therefore not clear in my mind about the nature of the anxiety feeling. I felt that it had not really changed and that it was still there. But it must have gone by and large.

I was delighted when I realised this for sure several days after arriving home on the 14th June. So my trip had been a success.

It dawned on me too at the same time that I had had the miraculous healing in the confessional box. I was sure that this was relevant and that it meant that the angels wanted me to sin no more, even in a small way. I therefore think that I may have a conditional cure. The feeling may come back if I sin. I am Christ after all and I shouldn't really sin at all, and the angels have got to perfect me. I don't know how long it will last but I will do my level best to ensure that there is no reason for me to have to go to confession again.

I feel so humbled by the experience of the healing on the trip and I am so determined that I will be ready for whatever God wants me to do in the near future.

I thank Our Lady for calling me to Medjugorje, a place of miraculous healing.

I also reflected on the miracle and realised that it had originated in a feeling that had occurred unnaturally in May 2,000 A.D.. It hadn't seemed to me to be something that was medical at first. It seemed more like something that came from God. It just didn't feel like a thing that I would normally feel, and so this gave me the feeling that it had its origins in God.

Thus I sensed the possibility that the healing was God's way of saying that he was lifting my suffering because I was near to completing my work. I had written six books while suffering from this terrible affliction and it just seemed like God had been giving me a Cross, an extra burdensome Cross on top of my manic depression, but a cross all the same, so that I knew that I was in a struggle.

It seemed that the doctors had to all intents and purposes cracked the manic depressive illness in 1997 when they gave me a small dose of strong antipsychotic medication to take daily. I had had very few symptoms after that. And it seemed that God needed me to suffer in order to purify me. It was purifying and it was terrifying, and it came from God. I had no doubt about that.

I knew that because of the comical way that it began as a helmet that seemed to fall gently on my head and then quietly rise again. It was terrifying, as well as comical, but I knew that God was involved as he was involved in everything in my life. The actual beginning was to me a clear act of God.

So, in the immediate aftermath of Medjugorje, I also debated in my mind whether this miraculous healing also represented the healing of my manic depressive illness. That illness had also began unnaturally as a giant, good-natured conspiracy against me that had ended with the death of Cardinal Tomás O'Fiaich. That had been unreal to me and I very much believed that God was central to the beginning of that illness as he was central to the beginning of my anxiety sensation.

Nonetheless, in the case of both illnesses God had stepped out of the equation in time and left me to feel the full rigours of the afflictions. It may well have been the case that God was simply helping me to become accustomed to illnesses that I was going to experience in any event. But I don't think so. I suspect that God gave me both illnesses so that I could legitimately judge other people. Moreover, I would have the incentive and the motivation to judge others as many people had when they fell on tough times.

God knew that I would not function as the judge and the just warrior, the non-violent warrior, unless I had a certain level of anger generated by being regarded as a second class citizen. He knew what my response would be to both illnesses. He knew that I would find it increasingly difficult to be an accountant, and that I would increasingly begin to see hypocrisy, shallowness and duplicity in the relations of others towards me. He knew that I would soon be judging others, contrary to his son's teaching, but fully in accordance with the terms of his son's mission on his return in glory, as predicted in the Book of Revelation.

My books would serve as a sophisticated judgement of sorts, and they would become an indictment of our modern society.

I didn't need to go far to see indictments of our modern society. It was very evident from the fact that the two largest political parties in the North of Ireland were led by the false prophet and the Antichrist respectively. So I was on to a winner straight away.

Thus God needed me for judgement. And so he needed the illnesses in order to ensure that I was sufficiently motivated to give them. And I did give them – in my books, letters and articles – and little remains to be done.

So was I now healed of all my afflictions? The tablets had prevented almost all symptoms of my manic depression from returning and thus the doctors had succeeded to an extent. But I would rather be healed by God because there is a sense that the tablets suppress some emotions as well as the symptoms, and it is a little unnatural.

So I'm keeping my mind open to the possibility that this sinless state will prove to be a catalyst for the healing of my manic depression. It would seem to be a bit much for God to ask anything more from me in return for this healing, but one never knows. God may ask for something in return for healing my manic depression.

In any case, I celebrate his miraculous healing to date.

Nevertheless, I received the clarification yet again that my God was the same God who gave and took away some six weeks after my trip to Medjugorje in early August 2007. Not wishing to let me think that I looked untarnished by my illnesses having been cleared up, my God ensured that the root of a twenty-five year old crown in the upper front row of my teeth had to be removed because it was not holding the crown.

So I have to somehow wait for six months for dental bridge work to be completed. In the meantime I can either use a denture that doesn't fit properly or leave the gap. So either way I may seem quite affected. But hopefully it will resolve itself next January and I will look as if I'm back to my self.

The Lord giveth and the Lord taketh away.

Postscript

I have alluded to some of the complexities of the healing process at Medjugorje, as at all places of healing. It seems that God may not really have healed me at all, merely put an end to the suffering that he began years before.

The reality may be that people who suffer do so because God wants to give hope to those suffering from illnesses that there is a way out. So the real favour that God is bestowing on those he "heals" is the right to tell the world that they were chosen by God because of God's desire to help people who were suffering.

They may not have been given a cure as such, but they are in God's eyes worthy to carry a burden so that others may have hope in their heart.

I feel that the real purpose of shrines like Medjugorje is to emphasize the message of Jesus Christ. It is in fact this message that God is suggesting, when he gives healing, that heals the world and not the miracles.

In other words, if we obey and follow the teachings of Jesus Christ, as humankind, we will not suffer. Jesus came to take away the sin of the world and that means that he came to prevent us from developing illnesses. His coming suggests that there is no need for illness in the world, if we organize the peoples of our planet to share its resources and to plan for a future where all human beings are given parity of esteem.

My miracle, when I was healed by an American priest in a confession box, may be a metaphor for the message central to Christianity, that the less sin there is the less illness there will be.

That is the way that God made us. If we sin, as all of us do in some way, we become ill from time to time. God randomly chooses the illnesses, I feel, that affect us in certain ways, which often means that the best of people suffer because of the sins of the worst of people.

People who receive miraculous cures may, I feel, also be good people who suffer because of the badness in the world. Nonetheless, they are chosen people, chosen to witness God's grace and favour together with his power. However, they may also know that he exists with a certainty that other people cannot fathom, and that is the greatest gift of all.